DEDICATION
DEDICATION

I have often said I need to write my autobiography for my children, even if no one else is interested. As I proofread this book, I realized it is my autobiography. It's stories from my life, pieces of myself put down on paper, written memories of me for my children after I am gone.

I would have never done this if my beautiful friend, Linda Leonard, had not encouraged me to publish a collection of my writings. So, Linda, this one is for you. Your request did not go unnoticed. Thank you for being my biggest fan. I love you.

Contents

WHERE I COME FROM

Sleeping Double in a Single Bed... 2

Clouds.. 6

Momma, He's Crazy.. 10

Salvation and C. J. Riley 15

Easter, Daddy and Me 19

Twenty-Five Cents – The Price of Betrayal 23

Ignorance and Bliss.... Not Necessarily a Combo 27

My Sister's Name is Jenny Allen.. 32

The Ride.. 36

Cool 40

Planned Parenthood 42

Fathers and Other Strangers 47

The Joy of Christmas.. 51

Revisiting the House that Built Me 55

So You Think You Can Drive 59

Who's Your Daddy? 63

The Girl Who Wrote That Poem............................... 67

Continuity 71

Fifteen Miles of Memories 75

EVERYTHING I KNOW I LEARNED FROM MY CHILDREN

Children 101... 80

Gotta Go 84

Talking to God 85

ID Country Style 87

Kevin and the Creepy Crawly Things 88

And Here We Go Again 93

Nothing Like a Good Book....................................... 97

Little Brother 99

Dancing for Jesus 100

Flying without Wings 102

Just a Brush... 106

Who's Your Daddy?.. 108

Single With Children 109

If I Only Had a Brain.. 113

God's Gift... 117

My Daughter.... Myself 119

Pumpkin Love.. 123

It's a Long, Long Ride 127

Fifty Dollar Sweatshirts...................................... 128

Semantics 130

White Horse 131

A Girl and a Dog.. 132

Who Is You? 136

Journalist to the Stars 138

Good to Go 142

Follow the Bouncing Ball 144

The Spirit of Christmas 146

Home is... 151

The House That Jack Built 155

Burned in the Fire 157

SWEET SOUTHERN WOMAN

Sweet Southern Woman 160

Moving On 165

My Greatest Weakness 167

There Ain't Nothing Wrong with The Radio 171

Lessons Learned – Lessons Shared 176

Eating at God's Table 180

Getting Ready to Lift and Stretch 183

Good Sermon 187

Sometimes You Get a Dog 189

Discovering My Inner Booty 192

Message From God 196

The Right Call 197

Cantaloupes and Candy 199

I Think It's About Forgiveness 201

I Had a Dream 206

Blinded by the Dark 210

Just Breathe 211

Don't You Like the Cat? 212

Getting What I Paid For 216

I Wrote a Poem 220

Out of the Darkness 224

'Tis the Season to be Grateful.................................... 229

Santa Baby 233

Time to Dust Off Those New Year's Resolutions.................... 237

Randomness? 241

Soft Southern Winds 242

The First Time.. 244

Green Stuff 246

Miss Hallie, The Original Sweet Southern Woman

A Time to Pray 251

Potted Plants.. 252

Adults Only 254

Quarters 255

Accidental Flasher 256

Funny Little Sinks.. 257

Fiscally Responsible.. 258

I Know You 260

Patience is a Virtue 264

The Giggles 265

Good Times... 267

A Mother's Love.. 268

And That's How Traditions Get Started 273

Something in Red 275

'Til the End... 277

GOING GRAY

Three Steps Behind 282

Things Aren't Always What They Seem..................... 285

Crackers.. 287

Wrong Button.. 289

Getting in Shape 290

Have You Seen Her?.. 294

Looks Familiar - Hum a Few Bars 298

Einstein He Ain't 299

Directionally Challenged 300

Clocks 303

Just a Couple of Bohemians 305

Light, Water and Love.. 309

Jean and the Super Star.. 312

Bargain Basement... 316

Coexisting 317

Nice Try 320

Douglas Scissorhands 321

Old Dogs and Children.. 325

Me, Me, Me 328

Keeping up with the Kardashians 329

Date Night 330

Art of Distraction... 334

The Importance of Drawing Water 335

Living with Germophobics 340

Bra Burning 345

Alcohol 347

Good Music Will do That to You 350

I Fell in Love Again Last Night 351

Open to Interpretation... 353

Ghosts... 355

Virtual Reality 357

Fifty Different Shades of Gray 361

Indentations 365

WHERE I COME FROM

Sleeping Double in a Single Bed

I am bemused by the need of children today to have a room of their own. I had a quasi-bedroom when I was twelve and a permanent one for about a year when I was sixteen. I'm unsure as to its value even today.

Hallie and Weldon Burr had their priorities straight. They had two children and one on the way when they built their house. They didn't give a thought as to who was going to sleep where. They just made sure there was a roof over our heads.

My daddy and Uncle Jack Turner built a square house – no floor plans, no permits, no hallways and no bathrooms. Momma thought she was moving up in the world because she was living in a log cabin during the building.

Her new house had two bedrooms, a living room, one closet, no doors between the four rooms, and a kitchen with a sink. The sink had a drain that worked and spigots that didn't. The well out back took care of the spigot problem.

The den and the kitchen were in the back of the house. The front door opened into a bedroom with a fireplace. Watching the fire die down during the night is one of my most pleasant childhood memories.

I was twelve before I got a room which I could - with one exception and without much conviction - call my own. The exception being my room was the one Momma "put people in". Nieces, nephews, uncles, aunts, brothers, sisters, grandchildren all used my room when they needed it. My room was the communal bedroom.

When relatives came to visit no one batted an eyelash at the sleeping arrangements. When lots of younger cousins were included in the family mix, Momma put us sideways in the big double bed in the front room.

A night spent sleeping like this had its rough moments. Some of the kids were taller than others so their legs hung out over the edge and turning over was never on the list of options. We stayed stationary the entire night.

It was like fitting odd shaped pork chops in the frying pan. When you turned them over, they didn't fit anymore. So, a simple act of moving once we were settled in bed would have needed the domino effect to work, and, frankly, it just wasn't worth the trouble.

We were just thankful to be in a bed, because our usual sleeping quarters during special family visits were Miss Rosie Brown's handmade quilts on the hardwood floor in whatever room had the most available space.

This type of bedding was called pallets, a name contrived to make us think a quilt on the floor was more than...well...a quilt on the floor. Momma had to step over sleeping bodies just to make it to the kitchen.

Sleeping on a hard floor should have made us appreciate pillows, but they weren't the softest thing about our makeshift beds. Unlike the expensive, luxuriant down feather pillows of today, our pillows were stuffed with large feathers that had the quill still attached. The innocent act of turning your head during the night could place both eyes at risk.

In the absence of a space to call my own, I improvised. My room was an old gnarled sassafras tree in the side yard. If I became upset, which I didn't often because it was frowned upon by the establishment – the establishment being my mom and dad – I climbed into the upper branches of my tree and hid.

I watched my brother Julious and my sister Jennie fighting beneath me, looked at my dad sunning on our tiny front porch, and read big thick books while safely ensconced in my tree. I even played with little metal cars at its base, winding my roads in and out among the roots.

My tree also supplied me with horses to swish about the dirt yard and make-believe cigarettes like my cowboy heroes. On days when the sun was high in the sky, laying a steamy haze over everything, I even dozed off in my tree. I invented camping before they had a name for it.

Having a room in a tree in the yard was not as farfetched as one might think. When I was a child the lines between indoors and outdoors weren't as clearly defined as they are today. There was no air conditioning, so windows stayed propped open all summer and so did doors.

Only thin shields of screen wire separated in from out, and we kids never stayed in for very long. We hit the yard, fields and wood before the breakfast dishes were cleared and only came back in to eat.

Clearly folk's priorities have changed. Children today will never view life from the branches of a sassafras tree. But having to make my own space in the world I grew up in shaped the person I have become so much more than a room of my own ever could.

Clouds

I saw some beautiful, unusually shaped clouds on the way home from dinner Friday afternoon. As I looked at them through the car window, I remembered what an important part clouds played in my life when I was growing up.

I have described myself as a lonely child, but I think an alone child would be more accurate. I didn't really have playmates. I was allowed to walk down the road to visit my cousins occasionally, but my dad put my visits on a strict time limit.

My big brother was four years older than I was and had his own friends in the neighborhood. Though I sometimes shinnied up a tree to show up the boys who came to visit, I spent most days playing by myself.

My family didn't get a television until I was nine and that, too, was strictly controlled. I had never heard of a toybox, much less owned one. When all was said and done, I had to find ways to entertain myself – not necessarily a bad thing at all. Creativity cannot thrive when everything is provided for you.

And, man was I creative. I made paper people and all the things it took to furnish a paper church out of the pages of the Sears and Roebuck catalogue. My paper people sat on paper pews and sang from paper hymnals. My paper pastor had a paper pulpit.

I made dolls from the Maypops in the field. I pretended they were Chinese, because the tops of the Maypops looked like coolie hats. I also made dolls from the dry corn husks off the chicken corn. I played a cigar box guitar strung with different size rubber bands.

I even had a trampoline. Well a trampoline like device. It was an old rusty set of bed springs I found in the field. Jumping on my makeshift trampoline was more of a challenge than a real one would have been. I had to avoid getting my feet caught in between the spiral springs. I wasn't always successful, but that was part of the fun.

But what really allowed my imagination to take flight was the clouds. I would lie flat on my back in the dirt, fascinated by them. We didn't have grass. Daddy made us chop up any sprigs that took root in the yard.

The clouds provided a theater for my fertile brain. I didn't just look for shapes. I peopled my clouds with all sorts of magical creatures. Clouds were my escape, my inspiration, the location of Heaven, that mystical place my daddy, a Baptist preacher, told me we would live in one day.

We didn't travel much either. My family usually stayed within a fifteen-mile radius of our small town. Once in a great while Momma drove us to Greensboro to visit my grown sister or to Kannapolis to visit my aunt and uncle.

Except for once or twice a year, my entire world consisted of anywhere I could walk, anything I could climb up, crawl under or crawl on top of that made up our yards and the fields and woods surrounding our house. That was reality. But the clouds, those wonderful clouds, provided fodder for my dreams.

One day, for a reason I will never know because the participants are long gone, my Uncle Bruce and Aunt Sarah took my family to the mountains. I was sitting by the window in the back seat, unnoticed by the grownups, as usual, when Uncle Bruce said, "Okay, Jean, I'm taking you into the clouds."

What! I perked up. The Clouds! My dream places. My little girl heart was beating so fast, I could hardly contain my excitement. But I did, because children were seldom seen and NEVER heard in my era.

"Look! There they are," Uncle Bruce said. I could hear the smile in his voice. He was happy to be showing me the clouds.

I looked out the window and saw nothing but fog. FOG! Just as I contained my excitement at finally getting to see the place that had fueled my imagination for so long, I also contained the disappointment of seeing the clouds for what they really were – fog, nothing else.

Jean, the little girl, learned a valuable lesson, perhaps a necessary lesson, about life that day. Still I can't help but feel sorry for that little girl me riding into the clouds in her uncle's car. Sometimes, maybe dreams, like faith, should remain "the substance of things hoped for – the evidence of things not seen"

Momma, He's Crazy

That old saying Children should be seen and not heard never applied in the household I grew up in. Children should not be seen or heard better describes my day-to-day interactions or, more accurately, non-interactions with adults.

Unlike today's children, my siblings and I never participated in grown-up conversations, nor were we consulted on any decisions, major or minor, even those including us. Children's opinions weren't needed or asked for. In fact, children weren't allowed to have an opinion.

Children and grown-ups were like gangs in a turf war - we tried to never occupy the same space. When company came we were sent outside, weather permitting. If weather didn't permit, the grown-ups stayed in the front room while we were sent to a different room.... with the door closed between us.

We were expected to entertain ourselves, too. And not by watching television. That would have disturbed the grown-up conversation. I whiled away many a night sitting on the kitchen floor rolling a ball back and forth with my brother and whatever random kids came with the guests.

The gap between the generations was wide and both sides maintained it religiously. The adults gave us information sparingly, on a need to know basis and, believe me, they didn't think we needed to know much. And we responded in kind.

Take injuries for example. Most were reported to the second in command - momma – unless we were involved in something they didn't need to know about when the injury occurred. In that case, we administered emergency medical care ourselves. If you were too small to make this decision on your own, the older kids made it for you.

My earliest memory of this imperialism is before I started school. I tagged along with the older kids and joined them in ditch jumping. My legs were too short, and I landed in the ditch on a broken mason jar.

Lest he be blamed for it, my brother Julious carried me on his back for days. Thanks to his vigilance, my parents never noticed I had slit the bottom of my foot wide open.

For the injuries momma knew about and other run of the mill illnesses, the shelves in the bathroom were filled with remedies. Turpentine was momma's miracle cure. The coarse oiliness of it soothed the hurt and momma tied a piece of old sheet around it.

We wore those homemade bandages proudly like soldiers who

had survived a battle. I never saw a band-aid until I was grown with children of my own. For major injuries she brought out the iodine. I think she saw the burning process as the representation of great healing at work.

Even though physical ailments were addressed and tolerated, mental ailments were unheard of. Those never got a foot in the door. My parents cared if we were physically healthy, but they would have scoffed at the word depression. That was something that happened in the thirties, and they had survived it.

On the other hand, outright crazy was common place. Dementia, Alzheimer's, schizophrenia, manic depressiveness, alcoholism, postpartum depression, and metal plates in the head were all dumped into the same category - crazy.

When someone exhibited outrageous behavior, it was glossed over with the he or she's just crazy explanation. Exceptions were made for those who only occasionally fell into bad company or housewives who suffered from bad nerves.

Once in a blue moon our normally hard-working neighbor would ride off with his brother-in-law, who people had categorized as crazy years before, due to an affinity for the demon liquor.

On these occasions family, friends, and any other adult nosey enough to join them - which pretty much encompassed the whole neighborhood - would wait in the poor man's yard for his return.

Kids were excluded from this vigil, but on one occasion we were in the trees when the gathering started. We kept silent, grateful for this glimpse into the intervention and retribution process of the adult world.

When the poor man finally did come home, his yard and porch were filled with people. They were sitting in the gliders, on the steps, at the picnic table, and on the ground. We, of course, were clinging breathlessly to our tree limbs.

Do you know what they did? They shunned him. Two hours of sitting in a tree and that was all we got. Everyone averted their eyes when he stumbled into the yard. The brother-in-law scurried off, and the sheep who had strayed from the fold was ushered into the house, not lovingly either, by his wife.

I don't regret learning to live by my parents' suck-it-up approach. I turned out to be a reasonably normal - mind you, there are some who would argue that point - happy, productive adult.

Devastating emotional illness aside, I think we average folk could learn a lot from the brush your hair, put a smile on your face and keep on walking attitude of my childhood. Fix what's wrong, and if you can't, then embrace your craziness. It just might keep you sane.

Salvation and C. J. Riley

Most Saturday nights will find me listening to reruns of the Grand Ole Opry on AM radio while traveling home from a gig. My father was a Missionary Baptist preacher with a penchant for fire and brimstone, but his first love was music, and I grew up listening to the Grand Ole Opry.

Country and bluegrass was the Opry's fare, but around our house gospel reigned. Daddy was a member of a gospel quartet, and on Saturday nights they would meet to practice. Even at my age, I loved the ambience created by those musically talented people.

My family couldn't go to church every Sunday because my father suffered from rheumatoid arthritis, a crippling disease. Eventually, this condition forced him to retire from the quartet, but he still sang solo from time to time.

Oakland Baptist Church at revival time is where my memory finds him, standing behind the podium, looking over his glasses at the congregation while singing *When They Ring Those Golden Bells*, his audience responding with enthusiastic amen's.

The assembled worshipers, wearing their Sunday clothes in the middle of the week, hoped to see the salvation of some of the community's worst sinners on those numinous nights of summer revival.

The lack of air conditioning did not dim the enthusiasm of the crowd as the choir sang one rousing hymn after another, accompanied by one of the Rivers girls. Mr. Jack and Mrs. Doris Rivers gave the church what seemed like an endless supply of pianists.

The screenless windows were raised in hopes of catching a hot summer breeze. Bugs flew in, attracted by the domed lights, and mothers rubbed the sweaty hair off the foreheads of their little ones.

When the pastor, Reverend C. J. Riley walked to the podium, the congregation became immediately attentive. He needed no microphone to magnify his distinctive voice as he read the selected scripture and led the believers in prayer.

Reverend Riley spoke quietly, but still managed to convey to his audience they were in danger of imminent death, and the words they were about to hear their only chance of survival.

The church was a venerable place, and everyone dressed appropriately. Even the farmers just leaving the fields. wet-combed their hair and put on their Sunday best. My father always wore a cardboard-stiff white shirt with his blue pinstripe suit, shiny in spots from age.

My mother donned patent leather pumps and her red Sunday skirt. A tiny bit of lacy white slip peeked out of the slit in the back, but she didn't seem to mind. My brother's hair was slicked down like Alfalfa's, and in my little girl eyes my older sister, Jenny, looked beautiful no matter what she wore.

My favorite outfit was a hand-me-down navy sailor suit with a pleated skirt. The matching top had a wide, white collar and red sailor's tie. My shoes had straps that could be worn behind your heels or across your feet, but there was only one option for me. I would lose them unless they were strapped on.

Reverend Riley may have been a quiet man, but not so the visiting evangelist. He screamed, he shouted, he begged, sometimes shaking his bible in the air for emphasis. The summer heat eventually forced him to shed his coat, and he wiped the sweat from his face with a large white handkerchief, voice hoarse from his impassioned pleas.

Unaffected by this grown up drama, I lay dozing in my mother's lap, waking only when the preacher became overly exuberant, while she cooled me with a cardboard fan donated to the church by Miller-Rivers Funeral Home.

As the crowd sang all five verses of *Just as I Am* for the third time, remorseful sinners came forward to confess their transgressions. The pious gathered around the altar to pray fervently for the salvation of these errant souls while loved ones watched in happy disbelief.

Alas, I grew too old to lie in Momma's lap, and Reverend Riley took his message to other congregations. Those hot, sultry nights of the fifties are but a dim memory. Though the tradition continues, everything has changed.

In order to adapt to a diversified society, today's revivals are shorter and seem tame in comparison to the ones I remember from my childhood. I sometimes find myself nostalgic for those intense, electrifying services.

However, honoring God is never a bad thing, no matter what format a person chooses. I am glad revival services remain a part of our church life, though I know we will never return to the fervent worship of those long-ago days at Oakland Baptist Church in rural South Carolina.

On the other hand, wouldn't you agree our world is desperately in need of some of Reverend C. J. Riley's brand of down-home salvation?

Easter, Daddy and Me

In the house I grew up in, Easter revolved around church. Period. It was not considered a time for frivolity. My father - and I know this will be difficult for some of you to believe - was a Missionary Baptist preacher who leaned toward the "put the fear of the Lord into them" method of raising children.

Heaven forbid, and I use that term literally, a child of his believe in a giant bunny who went around delivering Easter baskets full of unnecessary things. One exception was made - Easter biddies, baby chickens with pastel colored feathers that could be bought for a quarter at the local feed and seed store.

Easter biddy purchases were a justified expenditure, because by the time the color grew out of his feathers, the grown-up chick would take his place in the Sunday dinner queue. Each Easter I was allowed to purchase a new biddy to replace the one we had eaten.

My dad taught my siblings and me God would get you if you strayed from the teachings of the good book. These teachings were presented to us in adages, some directly biblical, some just biblically inspired. Honor your parents; idle hands are the devil's workshop; spare the rod and spoil the child; as you sow, so shall you reap are just a few of the hundreds I was raised on.

I adhered strictly to the rules at home, but Daddy didn't get to attend church often because of crippling arthritis. Sometimes I managed to skate close to the edge when he wasn't there to supervise.

When you're a kid, you must straddle the fence to be cool. My fence was the back pews of Oakland Baptist Church. When I sat back there with the other kids during summer nights, I managed to refrain from climbing out of the unscreened windows with them during the service.

But Easter communion was problematic for me. I was not baptized into the church until I was a young teen and Communion in our church was for baptized believers only. The other kids had no problem with taking communion before they were baptized, but they had not been raised by my dad.

I was twelve before I got up enough nerve to take a glass and wafer from the communion tray with the other kids. When the pastor read the warning that eating and drinking unworthily would be eating and drinking to your own damnation, the communion glass in my hand felt hot.

I looked around in panic. The kid next to me apparently hadn't heard the admonition. He licked the inside of his communion glass, saw mine was full and asked if he could have it. With profound relief, I handed it over. This would surely deflect God's attention from the crumbled-up wafer stuffed in my patent leather purse.

Religious child that I was, I began to worry my parents quarreling would get us into hot water with that stern God I had been raised on. Every time they started arguing, I would grab the Broadman Hymnal, turn to page 307 and sing *Just as I Am* at the top of my little girl voice. This only made them yell louder, but I don't think the argument had escalated. I think it was so they could be heard over my altar call.

My father passed away, I married, and became a parent myself, though not as taciturn a one as my dad. There was always time for frivolity in our house, and my kids had awesome Easter baskets. Those baskets were delivered on Saturday, though. Sundays were still reserved for church.

The year Tony, my first child turned two, my family met in Greensboro to attend Easter service at the church of my nephew, Mickey Smith. We were a bit late and waited in the vestibule while the offering plate was being passed around.

My five-year-old niece, Shellie, had my toddler by the hand and, not noticing the adults had stopped, she walked him on into the sanctuary. I waited until the taking of the offering was finished before joining them.

When I entered I noticed the seated worshipers were mighty interested in something up front. I followed their gaze. My two-year-old was stuffing his pockets with the money from the offering plates.

Stifling a gasp, I hurried up front to stop my little thief. Pockets bulging, he smiled up at me. Two years old and already he had grasped one of my father's adages - God helps those who help themselves. Daddy would have been proud.

Twenty-Five Cents – The Price of Betrayal

I was raised in the 1950's in rural South Carolina. My father, who was twenty years older than my mother, was of a Spartan nature, so our lives were not filled with amenities. Needless to say, the Easter bunny never left a basket for me.

But every year on the Saturday before Easter my parents would take me to Hurst Feed and Seed Store where for twenty-five cents I could purchase an Easter biddy, a baby chick whose feathers had been dyed in pastel colors for the upcoming holiday.

The Easter after my ninth birthday I acquired Tiny, a perfect little chick who would become my constant companion and end up changing the way I viewed myself and my place in the world.

Since I was only allowed to accompany my parents to town twice a year, this was an extraordinary day for me. In addition to all types of chickens, Hurst Feed and Seed Store sold supplies for most kinds of livestock. There were also saddles, guns, ammunition, plow parts, and even overalls for the farmers.

The smell of feed and manure assailed my nostrils before we reached the propped-open front door of the weathered store, and when I heard the frenzied clucking of countless chickens, I could hardly contain my excitement.

A smiling, bespectacled Mr. Hurst led me to where the wire cages were stacked and invited me to have my pick of the colorful chicks. At my father's behest, I usually chose the largest bird in the cage, but on this Easter Saturday, he was unable to make the trip.

Spying a tiny, pink biddy crouching in the corner of one of the cages, I apprehensively pointed to him. My mother must have understood my need to save him from the bigger, more aggressive chicks because, after only a moment's hesitation, she handed Mr. Hurst a quarter from her patent leather pocketbook. I left with the little pink chicken nestled securely in a shoebox under my arm.

Tiny was what he was, so Tiny was what I named him. I loved him with all the passion of a lonely nine-year-old, and he seemed content to let me. In years past I had forgotten my Easter chicks as soon as the color faded from their feathers, but Tiny was different.

My new friend slept in a box on our screened-in back porch and greeted me each morning with a soft whistle. He would come when I called his name, and often times he would jump on my lap to be cuddled while I hand fed him with the dry corn we kept for the other chickens.

Tiny even became attached to my father, and that was very surprising to me. I had never been able to attach to my father. I have a faded black and white photograph of the two of them, and the sight of that little chicken walking behind the old, crippled man still makes me cry.

It was a crisply cold, but sunny day in early winter when I betrayed my beloved Tiny. My father had begun making comments about my silly attachment to a yard bird. He said it was time to cook Tiny for Sunday dinner.

I was usually a quiet, well-mannered child, but I reacted with such rage to this statement that it startled him, and he sent me to my room. Not long after this callous and frightening remark, a friend of my father's, Mr. Linton, offered me twenty-five cents for Tiny.

Thinking I would be saving him from the dreadful axe, I reluctantly agreed to the transaction. As I walked despondently into the house with the quarter clutched tightly in my traitorous fist, I heard a chicken's frightened clucking.

Running to the backyard I saw Tiny writhing on the ground. Mr. Linton had wrung his neck. I was inconsolable. I cried until I couldn't breathe. But after his death throes stilled, Tiny lay motionless on the ground.

My father was pragmatic about the situation and, although my mother commiserated with me, she was too thrifty to waste a Sunday dinner by permitting me to bury my friend. I stayed in my room refusing to eat anything.

My father frowned on drama, so no soothing words were spoken to help me handle the crushing grief. Tiny was just a bird, after all, and I was only a little girl without any power. Moreover, the adults in my life, who were omniscient, could not be trusted to come to my defense.

Twenty-five cents was the price of betrayal when I was nine, and how sad it was to learn that it was my father's quarter. He had given it to Mr. Linton to purchase Tiny from me.

Ignorance and Bliss.... Not Necessarily a Combo

I am amazed at the things my grandson, Parker, discusses with his Dad. There is an openness in their conversations that was certainly not encouraged in my generation. I am a product of the repressed fifties, so his precociousness makes me a bit uneasy. But I am still of the opinion knowledge is power, and ignorance is at times far from blissful.

Anything associated with the male and female relationship was a taboo subject in our house, and although I was a very inquisitive child, strangely enough, my curiosity didn't extend to that restricted area.

Perhaps the memory of being slapped for using the word pregnant in a sentence stifled any questions I may have had later. I had to give birth before I found out where babies came from and, believe me, I was not happy with the way I acquired that information.

Having pregnant, one of my newfound words, removed from my vocabulary was a blow, but not a mighty one. There was an endless supply of them in my new Webster's dictionary. I had purchased it from the traveling Bible salesman for ten dollars, an exorbitant sum in those days.

It had taken me a long time to save that much money, but I loved words, and to own something composed entirely of them thrilled me. I had a dime bank when I was ten, and I begged dimes from everyone until I filled it. One of the shining moments of my young life was when I opened that dictionary for the first time.

One morning, not long after I bought my dictionary, I saw a word I did not recognize   scratched into the stop sign at the bus stop. While the other children laughed and talked around me, I silently sounded it out, but had no clue as to its meaning.

I puzzled over this new word all day. I knew when I got home I could look it up in my big, thick dictionary, the repository of all words. Imagine my disappointment when I couldn't find the word. I put Webster's back on the book shelf and hurried to find my father.

He was my go to guy for information, and I was convinced he knew absolutely everything. Unfortunately I couldn't get his attention because we had company, a visiting preacher and his wife. They stayed for dinner, and my grown sister and her husband also joined us.

Children were blatantly ignored when other adults were in the room, so I dared not speak out of turn. I waited impatiently for a lull in the conversation. Finally, one came. I seized my opportunity and very innocently spelled out my new word, waiting excitedly for one of the adults to tell me its meaning.

My sister swallowed something whole and ran to the bathroom choking. All eyes were on me for one very long tension filled moment. Then the world started turning again, and the adults resumed their conversation. It was as if I had never asked my question. The tape had been erased. How could one little word cause such a reaction? It only had four letters.

I filed the word away while the adults in my life, much like the government, fed me information on a need to know basis for the next few years. In our house ignorance was flowing, and continued to be cultivated well into my dating years.

In fact, before my first date, Daddy told me a confusing tale about an old pine tree and a young pine tree in the forest across from our house. I nodded my head when he asked if I understood and, keeping with family tradition, never told him I didn't have a clue.

Actually, what he said scared me so bad I wouldn't even let the boy kiss me goodnight.

When I had my own children, I tried to be more open with them, but some of their questions still caught me off guard. My second son, Kevin, inherited my love for words, and was writing books before he started kindergarten.

I bought him safety scissors and a small stapler. He cut notebook paper into lopsided squares, draw pictures on them, and wrote little stories about his illustrations. His miniature books were very primitive. He didn't know how to write whole words, but, bless his creative heart, he had learned the alphabet, so I spent my days spelling words for him as I went about doing my household chores.

One morning he was working quietly on one of these books as I washed the breakfast dishes. The word he asked me to spell this time made me miss a breath. He asked me how to spell sex.

Hoping I had misunderstood his request, I informed him six was spelled s-i-x. Impatient with my seeming lack of comprehension, he repeated his request. I spelled out the word for him, and as casually as possible asked what this book was about. He informed me it was a book about insects and he knew how to spell I-N.

My children are adults themselves now, and there probably isn't anything we haven't discussed. I am grateful that each generation grows more enlightened, and my grandchildren have a much better grasp of the world than I did at their age.

In fact, I think I'll have a talk with my grandson, Parker. I've recently started dating again. I'm enjoying it, but sometimes that conversation with my Dad plays itself in my mind. I need to see if Parker

knows anything about those pine trees.

My Sister's Name is Jenny Allen

During the first year of my marriage, the only thing I knew how to cook was a tomato sandwich. I fed my young husband Tony strange meals. I had no idea what ingredients were in something as simple as spaghetti. So, I just dumped Bunker Hill hot dog chili on it.

During this not knowing how to cook year, Tony invited his brother over for a chicken dinner. I rolled chicken drumsticks in flour and fried them without using cooking oil. Fortunately, I had one of those new Teflon pans.

After the chicken turned an odd shade of yellow marbled with charcoal black, I assumed it was done. I removed it from the pan and made gravy using only flour and water. The gooey mixture took on a life of its own and wrapped around the wooden spoon. I had to scrape it off and add more water.

My gravy then became white water with balls of flour the size of miniature marshmallows floating in it. The gravy would have matched the rice perfectly, except it was in even bigger lumps. My tactful brother-in-law refrained from commenting on the meal and even ate his portion of it. Nevertheless, I was married to his brother for twenty-two years, and he never ate with us again.

Most of my generation was taught from the time they could reach the stove how to cook entire meals. By the time my sister Jenny was a teenager she could cook as well as our mother.

I, on the other hand, was the baby of the family, and, according to Jenny, milked my position for all it was worth. Our mother's stock answer to my sister's complaints about me was, "Leave her alone, she's the baby".

I know Jenny held this against me because she spent years subtly torturing me. Jenny and our brother sparred constantly. Theirs was a no holds barred squabbling. As long as no bones were broken, and no one was bleeding enough to require stitches, my parents simply ignored their bickering.

However, Jenny and I were eight years apart, which meant she had to use the rubber hose technique on me so as to leave no visible marks. I am convinced some of the attention she lavished on me was just a cover.

Most of this attention centered on my hair. I always knew I would be going under the scissors when she cocked her head to one side and pronounced my hair to be too long. She would seat me in a chair, drape a towel around my neck, secure it with a wooden clothes pin, and "trim" my hair. I sat meekly in the chair as I watched most of my hair end up on the floor. It was getting stringy she would tell our Mom.

One fall she volunteered to make me look pretty for my school pictures. She rolled the ends of my hair and spit-curled my bangs. For those of you who didn't grow up during the fifties and sixties, she sectioned my bangs, rolled them around her finger, and secured them with bobby pins.

In my black and white pictures from that year I have varied lengths of misshapen curls hanging down my forehead. My smile looks a bit wistful. As if I were wishing my sister wasn't an amateur beautician.

Although Jenny's goal may not have been to torture me, the result was the same. When I was ten she decided I needed a permanent. She cut my hair extremely short before she permed it. Girls my age were wearing their hair long and flipped up or shorter and flipped under, but I looked like the poor man's Shirley Temple with three-inch curls all over my head.

Money was practically nonexistent in our household, so after Jenny married she still helped by buying clothes for me. One year she bought my school shoes. This was a big help to my parents, but such a disappointment to me.

Instead of my normal penny loafers I had soft ankle boots, silver on one side and gold on the other. The toes came to a point with a ball on the end. My sister must have shopped many stores to find just the right shoes to humiliate me with. I wore them the first day of school with green knee socks. I resembled a psychedelic elf.

We're grown now, but my big sister still won't admit she purposely abused my hair. I had dinner with her last week. She looked at me and said with a shake of her finger, "I had better not see my name in that paper you write for."

I nodded my head, but even as I nodded I was remembering those shoes. I smiled. Revenge is sweeter when served cold.

By the way, my sister's name is JENNY ALLEN.

The Ride

Firsts can be good, bad, awesome or horrific, but they always eclipse seconds, thirds and lasts in my memory simply because they were first. There are exceptions, of course, such as first day at school.

There are so many firsts associated with that - first day in kindergarten, first day in first grade, first day in second grade - it would have to be accompanied by some other event to highlight it in later years.

Of all the firsts involving school, it was my first day of eighth grade that stands out. It shouldn't have been memorable. Even though it was my first day of high school, as a sub-freshman I was beneath the notice of the real high school students. I was just moving to a different school with kids I'd been in school with all my life.

Still, it was an exhilarating time. Adulthood was fast approaching, and high school was the last step on that ladder to freedom. And my first day of high school was one of the few times in my life I was in vogue.

My older, married sister Jennie bought a tent dress for me. It was at the height of tent dress popularity, too, not a couple of years later, as was usually the case with my clothes. In retrospect, I think she was more excited than I was.

What puts my first day of high school into a special file in my memory was not that tent dress nor the kindness of my sister. Jennie and the tent dress were overshadowed by a wasp nest on the front porch. One ornery little fellow left the nest and flew straight into my face. All that exposed flesh, and he made a beeline - or would that be wasp-line - for my mouth.

Thanks to Jennie, I was extremely fashionable on my first day of high school. She even curled and sprayed hair. However, thanks to that wasp, I had a swollen lip so big it touched my nose. On my first day of high school I sported a stylish blue striped tent dress, beautiful hair, and a puffed-out sneer that put Elvis to shame.

One of my most memorable firsts was a car – not mine. My mom, in a moment of insanity I'm sure, let me go riding with Linda Rivers and her friend Tooney, the owner of the car. I climbed into the front seat between these two older girls for my first ride in a car without adults.

However, having been raised by my strict Baptist father, their exuberance made me extremely anxious. They yelled out of the window at people, honked the horn profusely and flirted shamelessly with the gas attendant.

Their behavior was typical teenage stuff, but I hadn't been brought up typical. I kept waiting for the wrath of God to fall upon us. I breathed a sigh of relief when that ride was over, and I was safely back with my mom.

On the other hand, my ride with Ricky Owensby when I was fourteen was a different kind of experience. Ricky was a relative of a relative. You know how that goes in the South. He needed a car, and my mom knew a man who sold cars. So, she hooked him up.

It was a beautiful sunny day when Ricky, his cousin Sally Lovingood - no it's not a joke, that was her name - and I piled into my mom's green Pontiac to go pick up Ricky's new car. I was just along for the ride. There wasn't much to do during summer vacation in the rural south, and a ride was a ride.

Then I saw THE CAR. It was a beautiful shade of dark blue with a black rag top. Just like in the movies, I moved in slow motion toward it. It took some pleading on my part, but mom let me ride home with Ricky and Sally. I climbed into the back as gracefully as Audrey Hepburn in *How to Steal a Million*.

Unfortunately, I didn't have that beehive hat she wore in the movie. As soon as the car picked up speed my long hair became a separate entity. I really couldn't see much of the scenery because hair was in my face, on my face, and wrapped around my neck.

Ricky may have spoken to me. Sally may have spoken to me. I heard and felt nothing but the wind. None of this dimmed my pleasure. Audrey Hepburn had nothing on me. I was riding in THE CAR.

For thirty miles I was in a world I had only seen in the movies, and I enjoyed every mile of it. Then Ricky pulled into the driveway, the wind stopped roaring in my ears, my hair laid back down, and once more I felt the ground beneath my feet.

I didn't get my own first car until I was in my twenties, and over the years there have been a lot of firsts in my life involving cars. I've been in a few more convertibles, even cruised town in a vintage Corvette one.

However, no ride in my life will ever compare to the one from Hartsville to Chesterfield in Ricky Owensby's blue ragtop.

Cool

Doug and I were watching a Smokey Robinson special tonight. Smokey sang the song *My Girl*. As I listened to it I was transported back to a sweet memory. I was fifteen, and an older boy had asked if I would go riding with him in his brand-new Camaro. I wasn't allowed to date so I turned him down.

The boy showed up at my house anyway. I was terrified my dad would think I had defied his dating edict. I knew I was in big trouble. My dad was not an asking questions kind of father. He assumed the worst and acted on that assumption.

I don't know if my mom understood me well enough to know I wouldn't openly defy my dad or if she just felt sorry for me. Either way she saved me. She told my dad the boy had come to show US his new car, and to take US for a ride. Quite plausible really because his aunt and uncle were good friends of my parents.

My mom then climbed into the back seat, leaving me no choice but to sit up front with the boy who had come calling without permission. Right before we circled the local hot spot - Moore's Drive In - she lay down, so it would look like I was on a real date.

My Girl started playing on the radio. It was the first time I had heard it. The boy reached for my hand and started mouthing the words of the song to me - a planned, romantic gesture that I'm sure he had used before. And, truthfully, back in my time it would have made a typical teenage girl swoon.

But I wasn't a typical teenage girl. I was raised too strictly to be typical. I jerked my hand back. I didn't like the boy, wasn't into cars, new or old, and had no desire to be circling Moore's with him. But I would wait until another day to disenchant him.

Because, at the moment, my mom, my sweet mom, was lying in the back seat of his car, stepping outside her dutiful wife role and risking my father's stern reprimand to give me a chance to go for a ride in a cool car with a good-looking, popular boy.

And that meant more to me than the ride.

Planned Parenthood

Mother's Day is no longer one of my favorite times of year. I used to "surprise" my mom ever year by showing up at her church alone or with kids and grandkids, and she always feigned surprise - year after year.

The surprise may have been faked, but her happiness at seeing us wasn't. Being with her family was always the highlight of her life. Now, she is happily ensconced in a world Alzheimer's created for her, and Mother's Day has become another holiday I try to avoid.

I thank God for my Mom. My Dad was a rigid disciplinarian, and her sweetness helped soften the harshness of being his child. Still, she was an old-fashioned wife and mother who taught her children the facts of life as she saw them.

Her extreme love for us made her overzealous in protecting us from life's pitfalls. She was constantly warning us of real or imagined dangers, and instilled in us a fear of dire consequences if we didn't avoid them.

Her most repeated warning concerned wooden, ladder-backed chairs, a furnishing staple in our household. They were in every room, even the bathroom. If she saw us using them for a purpose other than sedate sitting, even if we were lying quietly against the upturned chairs to watch television, she would yell, "Don't do that. Do you want to end up like Maude Garland?"

Maude Garland was my mom's cousin and childhood playmate. She didn't elaborate at the time on how Maude Garland ended up, but she did explain it to me when I was grown. Her explanation still makes me shudder.

In larger circles, Maude Garland is remembered for being the mother of Jim Stafford, the comedic country songwriter and singer, but not in the Burr household. Fear of ending up like Maude Garland haunted my childhood.

When the custom of women, to put it biblically, came upon me for the first time, my mom handled it like we were in the back room of a disreputable restaurant exchanging tainted money.

She closed the door to my room, and in a low whisper explained the whole reproduction process in two minutes...tops. The only thing I retained from her brief monologue was this mysterious unacceptable thing would stop when my body went through the change.

I was twelve and had watched a lot of sci-fi shows. The change, to my not yet fully developed brain, meant vampires and werewolves. Now a new fear was added to my long list of fears. When was I going to metamorphose and what was I going to change into?

My mom looked fine, and, to my inexperienced eyes, my sister Jennie seemed normal. In my mom's hurried and shortened version of our mother-daughter talk, she didn't mention this happened to all girls. So, I innocently assumed it was a random curse, and I was the only one in the family afflicted with it.

When she reluctantly let me go on my first date at sixteen, her advice was two sentences long - Don't let a boy kiss you until you're married. You'll end up pregnant and bring shame to the family.

Now that one made sense. I had never seen Momma and Daddy kiss and, since I was the youngest child, I had never seen Momma pregnant. Her inability or unwillingness to explain things in detail guaranteed I would interpret that advice literally. I married the first boy I kissed just to be on the safe side.

My parents were married almost five years before they had their first child. During the forties and fifties they had four kids three to four years apart. I thought that was pretty good planning considering the era.

I was expecting my second child before I shook loose the shroud of secrecy that surrounded adult matters and broached the subject with my mom. It would have been an unthinkable question for a single daughter to ask, but I was in the sisterhood of women now, and that made the conversation possible.

"Momma", I said, trying unsuccessfully to hide my curiosity, "When did you become an advocate for planned parenthood? It seems unlikely that it would have been a popular practice during your young married years."

Seemingly shocked by my question, my mom stared at me for several long seconds, blinking her eyes a couple of times. When she finally replied, I realized I had mistaken the look she was giving me. It wasn't shock. It was incredulity.

"Jean," she said in a tsk- tsk kind of voice, "I always believed in Planned Parenthood."

Wow... I was looking at my mom in a completely different light. My mom planned her family despite the societal pressures of her day. My mom was the bomb! How did she do it? Did she tell anyone or was it a secret rebellion? I wanted to know more. Eagerly, I asked for details.

Disappointed at the seemingly lack of intelligence shown by such a question, my mom sighed before replying, "It's not that mysterious. When we got married, we planned to be parents. We had no choice. It came with marriage."

Fathers and Other Strangers

I wanted to write a Father's Day Column about my dad, Weldon Burr, but when I reflected on my sixteen years with him, I realized I knew very little about him. My most vivid memories of him carry no depth.

He had white hair – he was fifty-three when I was born - loved paperback westerns, American history, music, and Beechnut tobacco. He had rheumatoid arthritis that couldn't be treated with the conventional aspirin-based medications, so he spent a lot of time in bed.

When he wasn't in bed, he was always sitting – on his red leather high-backed stool or on the porch wearing his red, black, and white striped sweater, letting the warmth of the sun ease some of the pain that was a constant in his life.

His legs, hands, and fingers were bent and twisted, locked permanently in a crooked, curled position. He was a musician, but those fingers could no longer span the piano keyboard or pick guitar and banjo strings. His musical expression was limited to singing, either alone or in a gospel quartet.

He shunned company, only inviting a few people in and then not often. He had no close relationships with anyone in his family or my mom's family, although he was respected and even well liked by them. They visited us, but it was random and always instigated by them.

In retrospect, it could have been his health, but I am not convinced of that. His grandchildren from his first marriage were the ages of my brother and me, and they were my childhood playmates. We were discouraged from having any others. He kept his family in that semi-hermit state he occupied.

He was also a Missionary Baptist preacher but, because of his precarious health problems, he seldom delivered a sermon. But he could not let go of the music. On most Saturday nights our living room was filled with members of his gospel quartet, picking and singing.

His musician friends and a man named Louis Streater were the only ones he invited regularly into our insular world. Uncle Louis, as we called him, was a black minister in our neighborhood. Even in those segregated days he and my father forged a close relationship. I was a preteen before it dawned on me that Uncle Louis wasn't my real uncle.

He was stern with his children and grandchildren. We did what we were told, and never - let me repeat that for the younger generation of parents – never questioned his authority. Disobedience was not an option.

My father was not my buddy, my pal, or my confidante.

But what was he really like. Before my birth, his debilitating disease already held him in its grip. A precocious, chatty child, I was probably an annoyance. Yet, he had the patience to teach me the rudiments of music, possibly because he sensed I loved it as much as he did.

He also taught me to sing harmony. He would call my mom in from the kitchen to listen when I finally grasped his teachings and could harmonize with him.

He was stoic. He accepted what life had dealt him with dignity. He exhibited no self-pity. It must have been devastating to gradually lose the ability to play any of his instruments, to only be able to tell me where the notes were on the piano, not show me. Still, Saturday night jams were a joy for him, not a reminder of what he had lost.

He must have been a kind man for one of my memories is of my mom telling him he just gave the neighbors our electric bill money and how were we going to pay it. When his brother died, he moved his pregnant sister-in-law and her children into the new home he and my Uncle Jack had built.

He must have also been a charismatic man. At forty he convinced my nineteen-year-old mom to marry him on their second date. Despite the pain he was in some of that charisma could still be glimpsed when he joked with my mom.

I would have loved to have spent time with my father as an adult. My memories are suspect because the brief sixteen years I had with him were spent trying to avoid contact with grown-ups. That was the typical parent/child relationship of my generation.

So, I mentally sift through the straw of our day-to-day interactions from forty years ago, and I find very little substance.

On the other hand, those few short years with him gave me a foundation for life. His code of honor was impeccable. If it wasn't yours, you couldn't keep it. If you committed the crime, you had to endure the punishment. If you couldn't pay for it, you didn't buy it.

When it came to morals, I was raised in black and white. I am also thankful every day for the fierce love of music he instilled in me. I married a musician, so music is a major part of my life today.

It's Father's Day and I wanted to write a column about my dad. He had white hair, loved paperback westerns, history, music, and Beechnut tobacco. He could have been the greatest man I never knew.

The Joy of Christmas

Doug and I were driving home from Virginia last week, and, during a lull in the conversation, I sat watching the rain-blurred stream of red taillights ahead of me. I wondered aloud how many were on their way to be with family for the holidays.

He didn't answer and before too many miles had passed the lights blurred even more as my mind started wandering down familiar hallways remembering holidays from another lifetime.

Memories are built around photographs, either hard copy still lifes caught on camera or random mental snapshots stored in our brain's selective file system. We seldom examine the myriad of days and years in between the stored memories.

We forget that the moments frozen in our memory banks represent only a small portion of our lives. So, as Doug drove steadily on through the rain, I tried to recall Christmas memories from when I was part of a family with my Mom, Dad, sister, and brother.

A montage of Christmas mini-scenes flashed through my drowsy mind. Little girl me standing next to the wood stove in long johns - a hand-me-down from my brother I'm sure - reciting my lines for the Christmas play at Oakland Baptist Church. My snow-haired dad corrected me when I made a mistake.

Red Luzianne coffee cans full of dirt holding the cedar Christmas trees upright. My mom's made-from-scratch Christmas cakes - orange, pineapple, coconut, and seven-layer chocolate with coarse, sweet, grainy icing. My brother tying all my firecrackers together, and the smell of my burning fingernails from waiting too long to throw those firecrackers.

My older sister, Jenny, waking me, then watching as I found my baby doll, fruit, candy, firecrackers, nuts and sparklers, smiling at me without jealousy or envy. In my family, only the little ones received visits from Santa, and she reached the age of no gifts long before my ability to remember.

Life in general, and Christmas in particular, was a financial strain on my parents. As an adult I learned that the extras to my dolls were gifts from various relatives. My stroller when I was five came from Uncle Bruce. My bride doll when I was ten came from Barbara Sellers, a family friend, and the tricycle I wore out was supplied by Margie Rae, an older cousin. My Mom hated charity, so I know it was love for her children that made her accept it at Christmas.

When I married and had my own family, I longed to give them the things I never had. But we were very young, and money was tight. The year our second child, Kevin, was born we spent the Christmas holidays with my widowed mother and my twenty-three-year old brother, Julious.

Kevin was only a month old, so all we had for him was a diaper bag, but we bought what we could for two-year-old Tony. On Christmas Eve we took the children to see the lights while Momma put the Christmas presents we had brought under the tree. I had wanted my brother to ride along, but he was working late.

When we returned I was happy to see my brother was finally home. He was the closest to me in age, and I missed him so much. Tony was carrying Little Tony, and I had Kevin in my arms. There was a little confusion when we opened the door.

The baby was crying, and Little Tony was squirming to get down. The first thing I saw was my brother with a huge grin on his face. Then I stepped further into the living room and gasped...audibly.

When my big brother saw how sparse our boys' Christmas was going to be, he went shopping with a vengeance. My Mom's living room was filled with toys of all kinds, including a tricycle and a big Western Flyer wagon.

Little tony ran from toy to toy with unabashed delight. While I stood trying to take it all in, Julious leaned over and whispered in my ear, "Yes, Jean, there is a Santa Clause".

The love of a big brother for his little sister overshadows the roomful of toys in my memory. And it is that memory and memories like it which binds all my Christmases together. Once again reminding me that the joy of Christmas will not be found in a trip to the mall. Nor will it be seen wrapped in pretty paper under a tree. It is and always has been in us.

Revisiting the House that Built Me

The house I grew up in was still standing, but its usefulness was over, and its destruction had already been scheduled when I went to bid it farewell. Tattered, sun-faded curtains hung precariously over randomly broken window panes.

The yard where we played our children's games was hidden by weeds... plainly smaller than the sparsely planted lawn in my mental scrapbook. In the ramshackle kitchen Daddy's cracked leather stool still stood, as if waiting patiently for him to occupy his throne once more.

Sadly, Daddy has been interred in the Oakland Baptist Church Cemetery for over forty years, and Momma is with him most days in her dementia- clouded mind. Big brother Derwood and sister Selma Rae have passed on, too, and those of us left behind are scattered far and wide.

Oh, but the memories evoked by visiting that tiny tarpapered, asphalt siding house with the crepe myrtle bushes, and climbing roses in the side yard. The three of us who grew up there never owned a toy box, bicycle, or any kind of mechanical toys.

Our ponies were slender green branches cut from the trees that surrounded our house. I loved to see the swath my ride's "tail" cut in the sandy front yard as I reined him in by his tobacco string halter. A sassafras twig was my cigarette, just like the real cowboys.

Sometimes I abandoned my cowgirl character to become an Indian with a headdress of chicken feathers. And, occasionally, if I searched hard enough, a hawk feather for the piece de resistance. The same trees that provided my ponies offered up a bow stave and an unlimited supply of arrows.

Notches were cut in the arrows with my brother's pocket knife, a staple for all little Southern boys in those days. Tobacco string connected the ends of the bow stave. My uncle grew tobacco. We found all sorts of uses for that string.

There was always a swing of some kind hanging from one of the trees, with a wooden board or tire for a seat. We stood on old barrels and walked them around the yard trying to keep the spinning from throwing us off.

Stilts were made from the tallest tin cans we could find in the trash. We tied, yes, you guessed it, tobacco string through them, stood on top of the cans, and lifted our feet with the strings.

Sometimes we nailed pieces of wood to tobacco sticks for another makeshift stilt toy, which never held our weight for very long. When

Momma had new linoleum put down in the kitchen, we used the cardboard tubing for a unique kind of stilt.

Almost every household with children had a western flyer wagon. Old and rusted, you could hardly tell ours had been red at one time. We would give each other a push and the pushee would go flying down the hill, speed depending on the power of the pusher. Those of us tired of waiting our turn would roll up inside a tubeless tire. It had more momentum than the wagon with very little pushing required.

Most afternoons would find the neighborhood children in someone's field playing baseball. We managed to acquire real bats, but our balls were made from tobacco string rolled around itself until it reached the size of a normal baseball, then covered with electrical tape which gradually came off over a period of time.

These homemade balls flew through the air with black tape tails trailing behind. I played outfield because I wasn't very good at the game. I whiled away many an afternoon, chewing on sour weed as the ball landed somewhere near me, and the kids on my team yelled at me.

Jumping was a big part of our entertainment. We jumped rope, jumped hurdles, jumped in leaf covered ditches, jumped over ditches, jumped out of trees, and even jumped off the roof of the house.

Climbing was a necessary companion to jumping. We climbed on everything. We even climbed into the steering wheel and spun back and forth. Once my Mom had to talk my niece, Verenda, off the barn. She could have climbed down, but she was afraid of the punishment awaiting her at the end of the descent.

Games we had in abundance, but no attachments, batteries, or adaptors were required. In fact, most of our games stood alone. Dodge ball, Hide-and-Go-Seek, Hopscotch, Kickball, No Ghosts Out Tonight, Simon Says, Ball and Jacks, Farmer in the Dell, Freeze Tag, Hot Potato, Mother May I, Marbles, Territory, Ring Around the Roses, and Drop the Handkerchief were all action games.

Memories filled my mind as I turned for one last look before I left. My Daddy and Uncle Jack raised the house. Now someone was coming to raze it. Similar words, different meanings. Homonyms, antonyms - the beginning and ending contained in one word.

Neglected and unused the house stood decaying in the sun. Visiting it had sent my mind rambling down long gone, familiar halls. I had a fleeting wish we could all still be there – together - securely within its timeless parameters. For the house had weathered life much better than we had done.

So You Think You Can Drive

Driving before we had a license or even a learner's permit was common when I was growing up. A rite of passage in my family was driving to Chuck Lear's store on the back roads when we were young teens. Momma, the licensed owner of our car, sent us off with Daddy in the passenger seat.

What innocence. Physical disabilities would have kept him from driving even if he had a license...which he didn't. One shudders at the thought of what it would mean today to get caught in a situation like that.

Daddy bent the rules a bit with me when I was twelve. We had ridden with my mom to drop my uncle's clothes off. She washed and ironed for him every week. Washing and ironing was not an option for the men in our family. That was woman's work.

While she was inside daddy, who couldn't work the pedals or grasp the steering wheel, had me get into the driver's seat. He pointed out the brake and gas pedals, showed me the gear shift and turned me loose.

I drove straight into the only tree in the yard. Seeing Momma coming, Daddy motioned with his crippled hand for me to get back in my seat. Momma looked askance at daddy, suspiciously at me, backed the car away from the tree and said nothing about the incident. That was a good thing because I think daddy would have thrown me to the wolves.

Once I had driven the back roads to Chuck's a couple of times I gave it up. There was no goal to shoot for. Even had I gotten my license my parents would have never let me use the family car, and very few teenagers had their own car then.

I was content to just ride. Alas, it was not to be. A few months after we married, my young husband had one speeding ticket too many and lost his driving privileges. One of us had to have a license, so I studied the book, passed the written test and got my permit.

Two weeks later, without practicing at all, I took the driving test. The fact is I couldn't drive...period. When the officer gave me a command, I would search his face trying to get a clue as to what he meant. I had never heard of most of the things he assumed I knew.

The officer did explain, albeit vaguely, what a three-point turn was. I tried. I really did. Five turns into my three-point turn, he told me to stop. I slammed on brakes. My sudden stop caught the officer by surprise. He came within a couple of inches of the windshield but retained his stone-faced demeanor through it all.

When we arrived back at the DMV, I looked apprehensively at the parallel parking area. The officer didn't even try to soft-soap it. He told me there was no need to parallel park because I wouldn't be getting my license that day.

I practiced and passed on my second attempt, but I never actually drove. My husband squashed me into the driver's side door and put his left arm around my scrunched-up shoulders. From this position he could work the pedals and steering wheel without too much discomfort....to him.

My own discomfort was not a consideration. Bucket seats were not standard, and two young people cuddled up to each other in the front seat was a common sight. The only thing required of me was to hold the steering wheel when he changed gears.

Although I was a licensed driver who never drove, I was still disappointed when I lost my license on my nineteenth birthday. I was raised to think the man of the house knew best. I knew I had been given some misinformation when I looked at that stern highway patrolman standing on my porch holding out his hand for my driver's license.

We had transferred our car into my name, and the man of the house told me I had ten days to get insurance. I didn't. Although this incident enlightened me somewhat, it was sometime in the eighties before I quit believing in that man of the house knowing best stuff.

Despite my shaky beginnings, I turned out to be a responsible, safe driver. I obeyed all the traffic laws and only worked my way up to going the posted speed limit when I noticed people were passing me on hills, bridges, and double yellow lines.

I couldn't have other drivers risking their lives to get around me. I also quit backing up and re-stopping when I inadvertently ran a stop sign. And, in all my years of driving, I was involved in only one vehicular collision. It was raining, and I hit a boat. Seems appropriate, don't you think?

Still, I don't like driving. I hate interstates and big city traffic. I love the back roads of the small Southern town I learned to drive in...well sort of learned to drive in. I drive because I have to, but the truth is I would be happier being chauffeured like Miss Daisy. Trouble is Doug absolutely refuses to sit in the front seat by himself.

Who's Your Daddy?

My first date was with one of the Smith boys - there were four of them. The Smith boys hadn't been in town long. My dad was suspicious of people from Pageland, so telling him my prospective date was from Florida almost put paid to the date before it began.

However, I really wanted to date this Smith boy. He had the cutest accent. And he had a car. In my teenage world the car alone would have been enough reason to say yes to his invitation, but the accent sealed the deal.

Fortunately, there was a saving grace - his mother had ties to Chesterfield. My dad knew of the family, but the stakes were high. I was his youngest child, and this was my first date. He had to be sure he wasn't putting me in the car with a miscreant.

My dad did what we have always done in the South. He asked around. The first question where I come from when you meet someone new is, "Where are you from?" The second question is, "Who's your daddy...your momma...your grandpa...your grandma?"

It was my Aunt Pearlie who eventually cleared the way for my long awaited first date. My daddy found out someone he didn't know, the

Smith boy, was related to someone he did know. Pearlie's daughter-in-law was sister to the Smith boy's mother.

Pearlie told my dad she had never heard anything bad about this Smith boy, and with that, the Southern town research team had accomplished its purpose. Daddy was satisfied, and I was permitted to get in the car with the Smith boy.

My son says you can't swing a cat by the tail in a small southern town without hitting ten people you're kin to. My son could be right. This makes dating a roll of the dice if you stay in the same town or even the same county.

That Smith boy eventually became my husband. Even though we were related to the same people, we weren't related to each other, so our children turned out fine.

Years later, after I had divorced the Smith boy, I dated a man who had numerous connections to my family. His sister was married to my cousin, his aunt was married to another cousin, and his uncle was married to my aunt. Though we shared first cousins through that last connection, we weren't directly related.

We forgot to consider that swinging the cat by the tail thing, though. After several months of dating, I was helping him clean his hall closet. "Hey," he said. "Look at this." He showed me a beautiful black and white photograph of a couple from another century.

I took it from him to examine more closely. "My mom had a smaller print of this picture," I told him. "She said they were her aunt and uncle." He grabbed the picture out of my hand and said in a pleading tone, "Please don't tell my children about this."

I was a bit puzzled by the not telling his children statement. I calculated the kinship in my head. I was about as related to him as I was to Johnny Cash - which wasn't much. I certainly wasn't on Johnny and June's Christmas card list.

Amused by his reaction, I set the picture on his dresser and started calling him cuz. He took the picture down. That stubborn gene we both inherited was probably one of the big reasons we didn't date long.

After I broke up with my "cuz", I traveled far afield when I started dating again. My husband Doug was born in Memphis, Tennessee. I knew my family had never traveled further than the mountains of North Carolina, so I was safe.

My daughter, DeAnne, went out of state, too. She married a man from Fayetteville, North Carolina the first time. Even though her dad's people were a bit more nomadic than mine, her close cousins were all accounted for.

I skipped the who's your daddy discussion with my new son-in-law. He was adopted, and although he was curious about his olive complexion and dark silky hair, he had never seriously searched for his birth parents.

Doug and I were having dinner with the two of them one evening, and we were questioning Doug about his experiences on the Nashville circuit. He had toured extensively, and we loved hearing back-stage stories about the country stars he had played with.

The table talk turned to how much my son-in-law and Doug had in common. They were both musically talented, both were artists, both loved history, and both even rooted for the same football team. Then my son-in-law, who was twenty-nine, jokingly asked, "Have you ever been to Fayetteville, North Carolina, Doug."

Doug, who had no idea of the young man's birth history, said "Sure. About thirty years ago. I dated a little Indian girl while I was there." Doug looked confused when we all broke into laughter.

He looked even more confused when I looked at my son-in-law and said, "Who's your daddy?" That cat's tail may have been longer than we thought.

The Girl Who Wrote That Poem

I attended Chesterfield High School when the rock gym was still standing. The school building was archaic even then. Everything was wide, the stairs, the hallways, the rooms, the windows. The building had no air conditioning, so the large unscreened windows were left open in the fall and spring.

Two senior boys put this feature to good use when a cocky freshman was bold enough to put his arm around one senior's girl - an extreme thing to do in the sixties. Each grabbed a foot, and, before he had a chance to apologize for his gross misconduct, said freshman was hanging from the library window.

I watched the event from my perch on the stone ledge by the gym. I was working on a poem while watching him dangle. That's what I did in school, at home, in the car, and on the bus. I worked on poems.

I was a loner in high school. I think my classmates perceived me as a bit odd. When we were older, one of them told me the only thing he remembered about me from high school was my poetry writing, said he only remembered that because it was so weird.

But it is the odd, the extraordinary, the hilarious, and the tragic that remain with us. The mundane, the ordinary, the every day events don't linger in our memories. I still remember the morning right before the home room bell rang when a tenth grader drove his car onto the grass in front of the school.

He slid the last few feet, jumped out, leaving the door ajar, and ran into the building just a few steps ahead of two policemen. All three disappeared from my view. It was the talk of the school. Not something you forget.

Then there was the first girl on girl fight I had ever witnessed, an absolute no-no for strictly raised young Southern ladies. I watched as the loser was hoisted by her slim, brown belt, crinolines flashing before being gracelessly dumped on the ground. It must have been autumn because there were leaves in her short teased hair.

All things considered I guess it really isn't so bad to be remembered for writing poetry.

Shortly after high school when one of those poems was published in Teen Magazine no one noticed. It was a love poem, full of teenage angst. I wrote it because a friend was in love with a boy who didn't see her, I wrote it because an older boy in tan corduroys and a forest green shirt never looked at me.

A few years later, when *Teen Magazine* was planning their bicentennial issue, they asked me to write a theme poem. It, too, was published. No one would have noticed that one either, but an amazing thing happened. High school yearbooks from all over the United States asked permission to use my poem as their theme.

Somehow the local paper found out about it. My mom probably told them. She told everyone, so I can't see her leaving them out. The paper did a story on me, and for about two weeks I was "the girl who wrote that poem".

Sadly, I did not fulfill my early potential. Mrs. Hough, my high school English teacher, was probably very disappointed. I did not become a famous poet, writer, or journalist as she thought I would.

Instead, I married the boy in the tan corduroys, became a stay-at-home mom, raised two children, had two more children, divorced, and raised those two children as a single parent. At sixteen writing consumed my life, and one day I laid it down and got on with life, as did we all.

Time passed. Members of the class of 1970 left home to get an education or stayed in Chesterfield to start their lives. We stayed in touch or lost touch. The eighties came, we raised families, we grew up, we grew apart. This decade finds us wiser, more mellow, and, though I hate to say it, old.

However, once in a great while some small thing occurs that takes us back to those glorious high school years when our future wasn't yet written, and we were a blank page full of promise. That happened to me a couple of weeks ago. Someone saw me on classmates.com and recognized my maiden name. "You were Jean Burr", she said. "You wrote that poem".

I have lived a lifetime since that poem was written. Only one of the yearbooks remains. The rest were destroyed in the fire that also destroyed everything else I owned. The boy in the tan corduroys passed away in 2004, and Momma was transferred to a nursing home where she remained comfortably oblivious to the past or present until she, too, left us.

However, for one millisecond, all those things fell away, and I was once again "the girl who wrote that poem" - young, hopeful, looking out over a brand-new world.

Continuity

My mom's father died when she was a young teenager. There were no government programs to help the pregnant wife and eight children he left behind. They lived a life of extreme poverty after his death.

Of course, there were no family heirlooms to hand down. But I did have a stoneware salt shaker that had belonged to my grandmother. When I held it, I felt a connection to a woman I had never known but was a part of.

The salt shaker was destroyed when my house burned, along with forty years of my own history. I no longer had anything physical to connect me to the past. And I think we all have a need for that, for a connection to the people we came from, for a place we belong, for continuity.

My mom had a tiny notebook that was her baby brother's. Joel died in his teens, after battling a lifelong illness. As a child I was intrigued by that notebook. Reading his words, I felt such an affinity for this boy who had lived and died long before I was born.

My grandchildren never knew my dad, Weldon. He died when I was sixteen. My mom, Hallie, passed away after years of suffering from

Alzheimer's, so they never really knew her either. Tony's children, Ashley, James, Jordan and Jayla, live near my hometown, but Kevin's children, Parker and Lexie grew up in larger towns.

When Kevin decided to abandon the corporate world and big city life to return to the small town he lived in as a child and young adult, it was a big adjustment for his kids. Fifteen-year-old Parker was told he could ride his bicycle home from town, and thirteen-year-old Lexie freaked out.

She said, "Dad, you can't just drop him off and leave him!" She had never experienced the freedom of small town life.

I empathize with Kevin. Although I love my life here in Greensboro, I miss living where people know I'm Weldon and Hallie's daughter, Jennie and Julious's sister, Shellie and Roni's aunt, and Carroll and Joyce's cousin.

Well, Carroll and Joyce are husband and wife, but it's one of those cases where they have been married so long, I forget which of the two is my actual cousin.

Unlike the anonymity of Greensboro, there are only a few people in Chesterfield I don't know or know of. Kevin, Aaron, DeAnne, Tony and his children have all experienced this, but Kevin's children never had.

I wanted to find a way to convey to Parker and Lexie the feeling reading that notebook gave me. I decided to take the two of them on my annual Christmas odyssey, honoring a tradition my mother started – placing Poinsettias on family graves.

On Christmas day I loaded my car with poinsettias and picked up Parker, Lexie, and their dad, Kevin. It was time to introduce them to the past.

Our trek started at the Smith Family Cemetery in Ruby and ended at Oakland Baptist Church Cemetery in Chesterfield where I told the kids, "If a tombstone says Burr, they're your relatives." They traversed the cemetery looking for Burrs.

The grave of my Aunt Nealie, who died in a mental institution, sparked a conversation on how being different from mainstream society in the twenties could brand you as mentally ill in the harshly religious household she lived in. At the grave of an ancestor whose stone had no name, just "wife of" they learned about the sexism of the last century.

Lexie loves the song "Hurt" by Johnny Cash and was thrilled to discover she and Johnny had a common ancestor buried in the Hurst family cemetery. Parker was amazed to find out my father, his great-grandfather was born in 1899.

Satisfied I had given the two a smidgen of continuity, I left them and their dad in Pageland and returned home to face a new year. While they may not remember everything they learned on grandma's Christmas odyssey, some of it will stick with them.

And I, too, learned something wandering through cemeteries with my grandkids that day. I returned home with this new insight - It is important to know where you're going, but it is equally important to know where you came from.

Fifteen Miles of Memories

I stood at the front door looking out over our yard as a gentle rain fell on the already soaked lawn. After living almost three years in Greensboro, North Carolina, I finally feel at home. I am comfortable with my house, my husband, and my new friends. It's not easy at my age to change your life, and it has taken awhile to adjust.

However, with all that I do have, I am missing a feeling of belonging to this geographical location. I am here because I know without a doubt I belong with Doug Palmer, but I have yet to become attached to his adopted city.

Doug is a transplant, too, but he has been here for thirty years. He was born in Memphis and, although his roots here don't run deep, he is still firmly planted in Greensboro. He knows the schools, churches, clubs - even the ones that have changed names multiple times - the best restaurants, grocery stores, dentists, and doctors.

All my contacts are back in South Carolina. Every few months I drive down to this place I was born. About fifteen miles out, I start to feel a sweet familiarity. Like an incoming fog, it wraps me in its soft mist, the gentle wisps growing stronger with every mile.

The feeling of coming home starts on the outskirts of Morven. Down a side road was a place called Robinson's Trading Post. I can still see my young husband, Tony, holding our first baby up in the air making him laugh as I search for a high chair.

Robinson's Trading Post was our furniture store. We bought our first kitchen table there for twelve dollars - they threw the two chairs in for free.

In the town of Morven, the house my dad almost moved us into is still standing. Like me, it's a bit battered by age. I wonder again, as I have so many times, if his decision to stay in Chesterfield altered the course of my life.

There's no way of knowing what effect moving would have had on me long term. Some decisions are made after agonized soul searching. Others are casually determined as quickly as the toss of a coin. Only time will tell which ones profoundly affect our lives and which ones leave no imprint at all.

I think my dad's decision to move to Morven was based on his love of the soft ice cream he could get there. We were too poor to acquire addictions, but that ice cream was as close as he came to one.

I saw the word chili con carne for the first time on the menu of that little ice cream stand. When something smelled particularly bad my dad would say it smelled like carne. As my mom ordered the ice cream, I pondered why people would want to eat something that stunk that bad.

When I enter Chesterfield, I am shrouded in anonymity, a North Carolina tag on my car. I pass T&C Grocery, home of the best ham sandwich I have ever had and Miss Hazel's beauty salon. I went to school with two of Miss Hazel's kids. As a teenager I thought her son had the coolest name I had ever heard - Rock Stone.

People, no longer living, drift randomly through my mind bringing a rustle of sadness. Tony, my first boyfriend, husband, and father to my four children dead for nine years now. My dad, mom, brother, sister, and many of the people I spent my childhood with are all gone - most in their allotted time, some way too soon.

So many places, too, are gone forever. B.C. Moore's where my mom bought my $1.99 penny loafers every school year was bought out, and Belk's, with its Bargain Basement, became an upscale department store and moved out of town.

The Peach Shed where my sister and so many others had their first job, Moore's Drive In, where you beeped your horn to place an order. The old laundromat on Main Street where, as a young married woman, I dried my hair and clothes at the same time.

Gaskins Skating Rink the social hub of my young life, has been razed to the ground. Chesterfield High School with its rock gym, custodian of my coming-of-age memories, exists only in the minds of those who left part of their past there. The shelves at Lear's Park N Shop, the biggest store my ten-year-old eyes had ever seen, are empty. Chuck Lear, too, has left us.

My home, my town, the place I left behind, receptacle of people I love and several lifetimes of memories. The place where my parents, and grandparents were born, died and are buried. I, too, was born here as was my oldest child. Four generations and fifteen miles of memories that will not dissipate

And so here I am in a brick house in a big city living my new life, a citizen of two vastly different worlds, but with the dirt of both clinging to my shoes. Greensboro holds me physically, but it has yet to capture my heart. That is still held hostage by a small town in South Carolina called Chesterfield, and forty-five years later Rock Stone is still the coolest name I've ever heard.

EVERYTHING I KNOW I
LEARNED FROM MY
CHILDREN

Children 101

The New Year has arrived, and as I reflect on my life, something I do on special occasions such as this one, I realize almost everything I know I learned from my children. Although, it was supposed to be the other way around.

But I was very young when I became a mother. I knew nothing about the job I had taken on. Not necessarily a bad thing because if I could have looked into my future as a parent, I may have cut and run.

I practiced on my first child and perfected my technique on the other three. Tony, my firstborn, was my guinea pig, but all my children have taught me different things at different stages in their development.

Tony was my accident prone child. I could probably get a job in an emergency room based on the medical knowledge he forced me to absorb. Thanks to this child I can handle broken bones, stitches that don't dissolve, knocked out teeth, uncontrolled bleeding, gashes in all sorts of places, and questions like, "Tell me again how your child stuck a nail in his head."

He also taught me to be very specific when asking a four-year-old to carry a project through to completion, because your notion of complete and the child's perception of complete may vary greatly. Once I asked him to dispose of a visiting baby's soiled diaper. He took it on the porch and set it on fire with Granny's matches. Children do dangerous things when parents aren't specific enough.

Specificity is important when dealing with children of any age. It's too general to tell two preschool brothers to take the visiting cousin outside to play. The visiting cousin cooperated fully when they spray-painted her. She even seemed proud of their artwork. But thirty-five years later I still remember that look on the mother's face as she sat combing paint out of her daughter's wet hair.

Here is a very important one to remember: Do not... I repeat do not let your friends use bad words in front of your small children, especially if the bad word is attached to the name of someone the child knows.

I was so embarrassed when the teacher circled the word in red on DeAnne's homework paper. She had used it in a sentence. Secretly I admired how well crafted the sentence was, and I have to admit I agreed with the statement. Nevertheless, I had to explain it wasn't nice to call Daddy's girlfriend that word.

One lesson I had to be taught repeatedly was never assume anything when dealing with children. For instance, when they're finally old enough to take their first shower, don't assume they're really cleaning themselves.

My son Kevin started taking showers when he was ten, but he just looked dingy all the time. One day I said."Baby, are you using enough soap when you shower?" His response was "I'm supposed to use soap?"

Even when they're teenagers you must not make what, with normal people, would be reasonable assumptions. Teenagers are not normal people. What programming you have managed to do on their brains is automatically deleted when they get that teen after their age.

It is most important to remember this advice when dealing with teens and vehicles. You cannot assume teenagers know how to use brakes, turn signals, speedometers, and most of the paraphernalia that is attached to a car. Except for the stereo, of course.

Girls 101 is a whole new class in parenting. Those tiny adorable creatures should come with handbooks. They make boys seem like a walk in the park. You can send a boy outside to play and he comes back in all grown up. Girls hang around you, talk constantly, ask a million questions, and, when you have a group of them together, they squeal and giggle. A lot.

Girls also need to know more things than boys. I never had to teach my boys how to shave their legs. When DeAnne was twelve I gave in to her repeated requests and presented her with a cute little pink razor. I forgot my assumption lessons and never bothered to go into the details of shaving. The poor child dug in... literally. Her knees still bear the scars.

A very important issue when dealing with the alien girl child is The Boyfriend. Pretend to like every boy she brings home, no matter what his hair smells like, how low his pants ride or even if you can't understand a word he says. Just smile and nod. They go away a lot faster if you use this approach.

Finally, know when to throw in the towel. Just when I thought the final bell had rung, and I could throw my mortarboard in the air and turn my tassel, the grandchildren came along. Since the kids I raised are raising them, the lessons keep on coming. I'm working on my Masters now.

Gotta Go

My husband Tony frequently left me in the car with our two little ones when he went in restaurants, rest stops or convenience stores to drink coffee on our long trips home for a visit. I was waiting in the car with them in some parking lot, in some city, in some state when two-year-old Kevin said he had to go.

By the time kids that small tell you they gotta go, they're pert near going. I looked at the flow of people coming and going and decided opening the door to let him pee on the ground wouldn't be a good idea.

I gave him an empty soda bottle and instructed him on how use it. It would have been fine, but Tony came back while Kevin was using his porta-john. That startled Kevin and threw his aim off.

I was sitting in front the front seat. The little pee-er was standing up in the back seat. The stream of pee transferred from the bottle to my long hair. I screamed. Kevin screamed because I screamed. Tony screamed because we were embarrassing him. Four-year-old Little Tony just kept laughing.

You wouldn't think getting soaked in pee would be such a precious memory, would you?

Talking to God

When my first child was two, my mom was engaged to a man named Charlie who had a very taciturn manner. Tony was intimidated by Charlie's gruff way of speaking and usually kept his distance from him, hiding behind me when Charlie was around.

One day we were having dinner with my mom and Charlie. Miss Hallie asked Tony to say a blessing over the food. Tony folded his little hands together, closed his eyes and started reciting the 'God is Great blessing I had taught him. Since Charlie was there, he spoke very quietly.

Charlie interrupted the blessing to say, "Speak up, boy. I can't hear you."

Tony opened his eyes, looked at Charlie and said in a timid little voice, "I not talking to you."

I had three more kids and taught them all to ask the blessing, but I taught them so young the only part they could repeat at first was *amen*. I had three boys, two of them teenagers, before I had my little girl, DeAnne.

When she was a little over a year old I had her lying on the living room floor changing her diaper. I was still amazed that after all those years God had given me a daughter.

I looked at that beautiful little face smiling up at me, always such a happy baby, and said, "Thank you, God, for my baby girl."

DeAnne heard the word God and recognized it from all those blessings we had said together. She responded by folding her tiny hands and saying, "Amen!"

My niece Shellie not only asked the blessing, she took upon herself the job of watching out for God's assets. Shellie adored my husband Tony, but when we went to an unfamiliar church for a gospel singing, she was unable to maneuver herself to a position beside him. Still, she kept an eye on him by constantly peeping around the two people who were seated between them.

When the offering plate was passed, Tony had nothing but big bills. He put one of them in the plate and took change for it back out.

Four-year-old Shellie missed the putting in part. She just caught the taking out part. Wanting to make sure Tony heard her, she yelled loudly, "Uncle Tony, you 'posed to put money in, not take it out."

Yep. We raised 'em right down there in South Carolina.

ID Country Style

Back before direct deposit, my husband, Tony, went to Texas with his dad for a week. On grocery day the boys and I went to where he worked to pick up his check. The receptionist at the front window was nice but refused to give it to me.

We lived from paycheck to paycheck back then, and I really needed to buy groceries. I asked to see the plant manager. She gave me directions to his office and told me to leave eight-year-old Tony and six-year-old Kevin in the lobby while I went back to talk to him.

The manager asked for my ID, but when I showed it to him he told me that didn't prove I was Tony's wife, just that we had the same last name. I was more than a little frustrated but kept my cool.

I left the manager holding my driver's license, went back to the lobby and retrieved the boys. I ushered them into the manager's office, said, "Tell this man who your daddy is."

They said in unison, "Tony Smith."

He gave me the check.

Kevin and the Creepy Crawly Things

People who know my son Kevin think he's not an animal lover, but that isn't true. He just likes the odd and unusual. When he was a child he became fascinated with snakes.

His father and I were sitting in church one Wednesday night waiting for our youngest son, Aaron, and the pastor to arrive at the amen of their joint prayer. The pastor made the mistake of saying, "Let US pray."

Aaron took him literally and prayed out loud, along with the preacher. As the noise of the dueling prayers ended, there came the sound of rhythmic thumps from the church yard. Members of the congregation exchanged looks and whispered comments.

Since neither Tony or Kevin had joined us when church began, mother's instinct kicked in. I slipped out to see if they were the cause of the ruckus. One boy had a bat and the other a shovel. Both were beating an extremely large snake unmercifully.

The scaly reptile appeared to be dead, and my children had disrupted service long enough, so when Kevin asked if he could keep it I nodded distractedly. He put the snake in a trash can from one of the outside bathrooms, and I hurried them back into church.

The next day the snake began moving, sluggishly, but moving just the same. His neck probably slowed him down. He was long and slinky as a snake should be, but because of the beating his neck detoured sharply to the right like an unfinished Z.

Kevin spent the afternoon "training" his new pet. Kevin thought the snake was cooperating with him, but what he thought was acquiescence on the snake's part was just a result of the injury.

Without my knowledge my well-intentioned son hid the dazed reptile in his book bag, so he could carry it to school. Leaving the zipper open so the snake could get air was a bad mistake. The snake recovered from his dazed state, stuck his head out to look around, and scared the heck out of the boy in the seat behind Kevin.

Kevin was suspended from the bus for three days, undeservedly so he thought, and the snake with the crooked neck was released into the wild. Several years later Kevin bought a python, satisfying that long standing need, but alienating some of his friends and family in the process.

When he was older, Kevin shelved his love of cold blooded creatures and became enraptured with the manatee. It's an endangered species in South Carolina. I know this because my capricious son placed a totally facetious ad on AOL classifieds.

The ad said we had a manatee for sale and had to get rid of it because it was living in our swimming pool, thus keeping the family from enjoying the pool.

My involvement in the whole situation would have been less had he not given his younger brother's e-mail address and telephone number. I don't think Kevin realized the South Carolina Department of Natural Resources monitored the buying and selling of endangered species. Apparently, it was a thriving business.

I was clueless when the South Carolina Game Warden called from Columbia to inform us he was coming to pick up our manatee.

"Oh, my goodness," I laughed. "We don't have a manatee."

"Ma'am," said Big Scary Game Warden "This isn't a laughing matter. Did you know it is illegal to have a manatee in your pool?"

"We don't have a pool," I replied, a little more subdued.

"Where are you keeping him then?"

After two days of conversations with the man, I finally convinced him we didn't have a manatee. I don't think it was my repeated denials. I am sure we were checked out because Channel 6 news got wind of it.

They called for an interview with Aaron. Their story was going to be big bad game warden scares poor little boy. Since Aaron was a minor, I refused the interview on his behalf. Kevin, on the other hand, invited them over, reveling in the confusion he caused.

My grandson Parker shares his father's love of snakes and has two as pets, but Lexie, my granddaughter wants cats. So, Kevin swallowed his dislike of the normal, everyday kind of pet and purchased a cat. They named him King Arthur.

Lex played with the beautiful, long-haired cat when she came over, but in the interim Kevin and King Arthur's cohabitation was uneasy to say the least. Unfortunately, the cat was able to pick up on the ambivalent vibes emanating from Kevin, so when he rubbed the cat... grudgingly, the cat would allow him...grudgingly.

Kevin and the cat tiptoed around each other for three years.

Last week Kevin's status on Facebook read, "My cat killed himself last night." Luckily an eyewitness was able to confirm his story as well as attest to the fact that King Arthur and Kevin had relationship issues, so there won't be an investigation.

King Arthur was interred in the back yard, with the whole family in attendance. Kevin was among the mourners. But those of us who know of his love for creepy crawly things still go hmmm......

And Here We Go Again

My oldest son, Tony, has always been accident prone - lots of emergency visits while raising that child. So many the ER staffers started making me write down in detail exactly how the accidents occurred. I expected the Department of Social Services to coming walking into the emergency room on more than one occasion.

I wouldn't really blame them. Some of those accidents were strange indeed. Like sticking a nail in his head when he was four. That one happened because he was playing underneath a hitching post. We didn't have a horse. The post came with our rental house. There was a nail in the top of it that was so long it had gone through the post and was sticking through on the underside.

I stuck my head out the door and yelled, "Lunch is ready." Tony jumped up when he heard that. I guess the child was hungry. That big, long nail stuck in his little head. That's when I learned my poor little boy was what old folks called a bleeder. Over the years the blood was scarier than the injuries.

Not long after the hitching post accident, Tony saw the neighbor's dog bury something. Tony got his little plastic shovel and tried to dig up what the dog had buried. The dog objected and went on the attack. He didn't try to bite Tony, just push him away from his hiding place. Have you ever tried explaining how a dog's claw got stuck in your child's head?

The accidents kept on coming. One Sunday after church Tony was jumping around the living room pretending to be a cowboy. He was using his Sunday go to meeting belt as a lasso. The buckle hit him in the head. My niece Sherry fainted when she saw the blood. With Sherry lying on the floor and unable to staunch Tony's bleeding, I had to call the EMT's.

I thought school would slow him down. Not so. When he started first grade, he was riding his bicycle while waiting on the bus. I don't know if he stopped too quickly or hit something in the yard, but he stuck the handlebars in his stomach. He started throwing up. No school that day, just another emergency room visit.

All those accidents turned him into one tough little kid. When he was seven he stepped on a nail attached to a board. He pulled it out before hobbling back to the house leaning on his little brother. The doctor probed it, said it had gone all the way up to the head. He couldn't believe Tony had pulled it out.

The accidents changed character as he grew older. His first job after high school, a piece of metal got stuck in his eye. Made me wince to look it. Then one morning he was working on his car at the bottom of the hill below our house. We were inside with the windows closed and still heard him yelling. The motor had fallen through the car and on his foot.

What he chose to do for a living was not the best job for an accident-prone young man. But he loved working with his hands, building things, repairing things, so found his life calling in carpentry. Although I had stopped being his chauffer to the emergency room, I made several trips to the hospital to visit him because of that job.

Those accidents landed him in the operating room more than once. He shot a nail through his knee with a nail gun. The nail lodged behind his kneecap requiring surgery to remove it. He shot himself through the finger, too, but just put electrical tape over that one and went back to work. He sent me a picture. I almost threw up.

And it's not just work. He redid my bathroom for me and was bitten by a spider. He kept on working, but after only a couple of hours the bite was red and swollen, already showing signs of infection. I took him to my doctor. Of course, it wasn't just an ordinary house spider. Tony had been bitten by a Brown Recluse.

The doctor had to cut out the infection and remove the flesh around the wound, too. After that surgery, Tony insisted on going to Walmart. I walked alongside him watching the oozing from beneath the bandage wishing he had listened to the "Stay off it" advice from the doctor.

I don't know if it's that innate toughness or the frequency with which they happen that caused him to make light of the accidents he continued to have after he grew up. I would like to think he's slowed down the last few years, but I suspect there were so many, he just stopped telling me about them.

My little boy is gray-haired now. He works with a company that travels all over the United States building and repairing chain restaurants. Much to my delight he was working a few miles from me a couple of months ago. I cooked for him and one of his co-workers. It was a wonderful evening.

I woke up to a text from him the next morning. It said, "That hospital in High Point sure is a good hospital..."

Nothing Like a Good Book

When I became pregnant with my third child, Aaron, twelve-year-old Tony and ten-year-old Kevin were delighted. On our weekly trip to the library, Kevin checked out half a dozen books on babies. As usual, he started reading them before we got home.

As I pulled into the drive, he was making all sorts of angry noises from the back seat. I was barely out of the car when he almost shouted, "Just look at this, Momma." I persuaded him to let me put my own books down first.

I wasn't apprehensive at all.

I should have been.

The book was about how babies are made, starting with roosters and hens, running the gamut of animals, and ending with men and women. It was blunt, but truthful.

"Is this right, Momma?" Kevin said accusingly. Not seeing an escape route, I swallowed hard and answered in the affirmative.

"Momma," he said, "Did you and dad...?" I never heard the rest of that question. I was already in the kitchen starting dinner before he finished asking it. I thought the boy and his mother had exchanged enough truth for one day.

Little Brother

My oldest son Tony was twelve when we found out I was going to have another baby. He wouldn't even let me lift a tea pitcher. When the doctor put me on full bed rest, he took over washing the dishes, cleaning the house, even grocery shopping.

When his little brother Aaron was born Tony was a doting big brother. He learned to feed him, bathe him and dress him. Unlike his dad, Tony had no problem changing diapers.

When Aaron was about two months old, we were having a family cookout. Our picnic area had been built in a spot that had a lot of trees. So small and larger stumps abounded.

Tony was walking toward one of the picnic tables carrying the baby and tripped over a stump. Though he couldn't keep from falling, he controlled the fall. He landed on his knees, then on his elbows, holding his little brother safely aloft in his hands.

When he got up, he wasn't worried about his bruised knees or skinned elbows, he was just deeply apologetic and near tears. He was afraid I wouldn't trust him to carry the baby anymore. What my precious child didn't realize was it made me trust him all the more.

Dancing for Jesus

My youngest son, Aaron, took a liking to religion. When he was four we bought a video camera. Our fourteen-year-old, Kevin, liked to film himself holding a guitar and lip-synching to his favorite records - yep records.

One morning Kevin asked Aaron to be his backup. He put a blue corduroy coat, sunglasses and a sporty black hat on his little brother and told him to dance and move his lips behind him. Aaron looked like a tiny Blues Brother.

Although willing to pretend he was singing, Aaron balked at dancing. He had decided, on his own, that dancing was not proper. He curled up in a recalcitrant ball on the couch and refused to dance. Kevin begged him to cooperate.

Finally, in a pouty voice, Aaron said, "Okay, I'll dance, but I'm dancing for Jesus."

He then threw himself into the music. In jacket, hat, sunglasses and underwear - Kevin had neglected to put pants on him - Aaron jumped and leapt behind his brother with a joy that was delightful to watch.

The decision to do it for Jesus had changed his whole attitude. I'm sure there's a lesson for all of us in there somewhere.

Flying without Wings

I believe in letting people, my children included, walk their own path without interference from me, but I was not always this way. When I was my daughter's age, Gloria Steinem's voice was yet to be heard in our small Southern town, and I learned to restrain my burgeoning personality to conform to the expectations of an inflexible world. My childhood was a tempered one.

When I had my first two children I was still hampered by family and societal pressure to be like everyone else. However, by the time my two younger children were growing up, I had been thrown into the world to fend for myself.

I had spent years distinguishing my inner voice from those of my parents, siblings, friends, and the world in general and summoned the courage to ignore the bridge-out sign they had placed on my life.

I jumped the ditch and forged a whole new road, taking my children along for the ride. As a result, I have reared four uniquely different children. No two are alike, and each of them is free to follow his or her own dream, not one foisted on them by a well-meaning parent.

Aaron, my third son, has always been the most subdued and less nonsensical of the four. He is a seeker of knowledge, and over the years has absorbed a lot of it. He is very patient when explaining things to me, but I still can't understand half of what he says.

His brain seems to be wired much like the computers he loves. For Aaron there must be logic. I first noticed this when he was three. He found a lighter and was trying to make it fire. I grabbed it from him and admonished, "You could burn the house up." His tiny brow wrinkled. Genuinely perplexed he asked, "But Ma'am wouldn't that be down?"

I guess you noticed the Ma'am thing. I taught all my children to show respect to adults by saying sir or ma'am. Aaron was confused by this, and thought I wanted to be called Ma'am, so he started calling me Ma'am instead of Momma.

Aaron's need for things to be logical caused problems for both of us with his school teachers. When he was in second grade, his school administered a reading comprehension test. One of the questions was *did Jonathan shoot the bow*? Aaron answered no, and the teacher marked it wrong.

Aaron came home from school so upset I had to schedule a meeting with the teacher. I took Aaron with me. My logical little man explained to his teacher that a bow cannot be shot. Jonathan shot the arrow. He just used the bow to do it. The teacher was so impressed with his reasoning she adjusted his grade.

Some people think logic and religion do not go hand in hand, but Aaron was a very religious child. He believed in praying. It was impossible to shake that child's faith.

When he was a few months shy of four, our car was totaled on a family trip to Charleston. My husband asked a car dealer friend to supply us with a cheap vehicle until we settled with the insurance company.

Not long after the wreck, Aaron was saying his bedtime prayers and asked God to find us a car. As an afterthought, much like a PS to a letter, he peremptorily told God to make it a green one. I explained to him we did not give God orders. Just having a car to drive would be enough. But Aaron liked green.

When his father called to tell me his friend was bringing the car over, I hesitantly asked what color it was. Upon being told that, yes, it really did matter, he called the man back. I don't have to tell you what color it was, do I?

Aaron always asked a blessing on his food with one eye open, thanking God for each thing on his plate. One day at lunch, he scrutinized his Kool-Aid with his open eye, and then rolled it over at me.

Putting God on hold for a moment, he whispered, "Mommy I

wanted cola." I whispered back, "We don't have any." Not getting the answer he wanted from me, he decided to go over my head. He thanked God for the Kool-Aid, but informed him, he really wanted cola.

After the amen, he put his faith into action and asked me again for cola. I opened the fridge to show him there was none. I pulled out ketchup, mustard, mayo, tea, Kool-Aid. Much to my surprise behind all of these was a generic brand two-liter cola. The older boys wouldn't drink it because it wasn't a brand name. I was stunned, but Aaron just smiled at my lack of faith.

My children are all adults now, walking, feet unbound, down the path they have chosen. I am glad they have learned from me that our spirits have wings, and wings were made for flying.

Just a Brush

My first husband and I built a beach house in Pageland, South Carolina. We lived about 130 miles from the beach, but I was attracted to the idea of living up among the trees I loved. A beautiful set of stairs led to our front door.

The narrow side porch led around to a large covered deck, which is just another name for a porch. The deck had double glass doors that led into our living room and dining room. Our family loved that house.

One day in 1988 I was leaving to pick six-year-old Aaron and his friend Larry up from school. Three-year-old DeAnne was playing underneath the house, but as I was getting in the car decided to go with me instead of staying there with her dad.

I stopped to buy the kids an ice cream cone, then dropped Larry off at his house. By the time I arrived home, my house was gone. And everything in it. And everything under it. And some of the things beside of it. It had burned to the ground. I had lost everything in that thirty-minute drive to the school.

My husband had escaped by jumping across the four-foot side porch, through the flames that enveloped it. Apart from a couple of boxes of papers that were in an outside building, we lost everything we owned.

Well, almost everything. There was a pink brush in my car. I sat brushing DeAnne's hair with it while we waited for her brother that day. I still have it. It's almost thirty years old, scarred and battered with embedded dirt that can't be washed out. But I cannot bring myself to throw it away.

We lost all our possessions that day, and not long after the fire we lost our family, too. To divorce. You might think I keep that pink brush as a reminder of another life, a life I had before the fire. You would be wrong.

I keep it as a reminder that my daughter is here with me because her last-minute decision to ride with me that day saved her life. The fire started underneath the house with the explosion of a gas-filled weed eater. Where DeAnne was playing. I have DeAnne. Everything I lost in the fire pales in comparison to that.

I keep that dirty pink brush as a reminder that God is good.

Who's Your Daddy?

When my oldest son, Tony, was seventeen, he had a little Toyota station wagon which was badly in need of a paint job. He sandpapered and primed the problem areas. But when he discovered how expensive painting it would be, he decided to decorate it instead.

He and his fifteen-year-old brother Kevin and their friends wrote all over the car with spray. He even let his five-year-old brother and toddler sister help. They couldn't write, so their contributions were strange looking indeed. When the crew was finished, they had turned that little Toyota into the ugliest car I have ever seen.

One night, after the haphazard paint job, he came home complaining. He had been stopped again. Although he had been pulled over countless times for speeding, he insisted this time it was because of his car. He had a valid point. I would have stopped that car just to see who was driving.

His dad, who had been listening to our conversation with one ear and the television with the other, was on his way to the kitchen when Tony got to the part where the policeman asked who his father was. He stopped, turned back to Tony with a horrified expression, and said, "You didn't tell him, did you?"

Single With Children

Being single with children required much creativity on my part. I had been a stay-at-home mom before my divorce, so having total responsibility for the children was not a problem. But paying the bills on one very small income was.

I cut everything possible from the budget, and then started examining the things I thought we couldn't live without. The kids had gotten used to eating, so I had to keep that in. What if I didn't have to make a car payment? That would be a major boost to my finances.

I decided to save money by purchasing inexpensive cars. What I found was when you buy cheap cars you get...well...cheap cars. It was like spinning a roulette wheel. In one year I had three cars.

Two of them only lasted a few months, but the last one, a Country Squire station wagon, required very little upkeep and was the safest vehicle I have ever owned. I purchased it for one hundred and twenty-five dollars. The children loved it, probably because it was bigger than their bedroom.

The Saturday before my son Aaron's ninth birthday we were going to the theater. It rained the whole trip and, just a few miles from our destination, we became the middle car in a three-car pile-up. Thanks to my old station wagon being built like a tank, no one was injured. The car behind me pushed me into a boat. Yes, it was raining. Yes, I hit a boat.

The next week the insurance adjuster came to examine my damages. He looked at the shattered back tail light, then walked to the front where a parking light had been broken. Since there was a dent he had to consider repainting the car.

He stood chewing his pencil and looking at the visible paint brush strokes and cat paws across the hood. Finally, he said, "Ma'am, there's no way we can match this paint job." He asked if he could just throw in some extra. I nodded, and he wrote me a check for five hundred and twenty-five more dollars than my car had cost.

Another problem that was impossible to circumvent was medical care. My ex-husband, contrary to the judge's ruling, dropped insurance on the children, and I couldn't get it at my job, so I tried to keep the kids as healthy as possible.

Then my teenage daughter broke her hand and had to see an orthopedic surgeon. He made x-rays, set the bone, and put a cast from her fingers to her elbow. I swallowed hard and paid the astronomical sum he charged for all of this.

Two months later, when it was time for the cast to come off, I was informed it was going to cost the same as when it was put on. DeAnne and I made the decision to remove the cast ourselves.

After trying several different tools, we settled on serrated steak knives. My daughter started at the top, and I started at the bottom. After almost three hours we broke through. The cast didn't budge. I had to call a couple of guys to come break it off for us. As they were leaving, one of them said, "Jean, I would have given you the money if you had asked."

Rent was probably my biggest expense. I even rented a house that came with a dog. Frisco was adorable, but he never let us forget it was his house. In a way, he was right. The rent was cheap because we took care of Frisco.

One night, DeAnne found me sitting on our rented couch crying as I watched Frisco play with his chew toy. Since me crying was a rare sight, she was alarmed. "Momma," she said, sitting down beside me, "What's wrong?"

I wiped my tears with the back of my hand before replying, "I was just thinking how sad it was to be almost fifty years old and have to rent your dog."

I am glad those days are behind me, but not sorry I lived through them. My children and I learned so much during those skating on the edge of poverty days. According to Aaron, the most important one was if you want something, you have to work for it. He said that was a valuable lesson for kids to learn.

As an added bonus, all those years of doing without turned me into quite a handywoman. I can install door knobs, replace toilet bowl innards, mow my lawn, and do most minor repair jobs around the house.

It's been some time since I've had to use my repair knowledge, so I'm a little rusty. But when my inside car door handle broke today, I grabbed a screw driver, took the panel off and worked my magic.

Now it's really broken. Until I can get to a body shop, guess I'll be climbing out the driver's side window like the Dukes of Hazzard guys. Yee-Haa!

If I Only Had a Brain

My oldest son, Tony, is almost sixteen years older than my youngest child, DeAnne, so I bought school supplies, woke children, got them dressed, packed lunches, paid tuition, and solved countless homework problems for over thirty years.

During those years I heard every last-minute request even a creative student could contrive.... until my third child, Aaron. My little sixth grader had worked diligently on his science project. Miss Woodbury was his favorite teacher, and he wanted to impress her.

Even at that age, Aaron was already setting high standards for himself. Still, it was a very challenging project, even for my little smarty pants. It was based on the theory that humans can control involuntary processes such as temperature, heart rate or hiccups.

Aaron, as always, was thorough and professional in his approach. He had to be his own control subject, mainly because he couldn't get the rest of us to cooperate. Amazingly, he managed to raise and lower his temperature and heart rate.

The day he turned his project in, he was very excited. However, when I picked him up from school his excitement had turned to frustration. He had to produce a concrete representation of his thesis. Aaron was convinced he couldn't provide one.

I had been soothing his tendency to panic since that day the dog ate his turtle, so I wasn't alarmed. "Calm down," I told him, "and tell me what you need." I was driving when I asked the question and almost came to a stop when he answered it. Aaron needed a brain.

Where does one shop for a brain? I put on my Super Mom cape and, like the scarecrow in the Wizard of Oz, went in search of a brain. Of course, the scarecrow was smart enough to figure out brains aren't sold on street corners.

I started with grocery stores. Aaron and I had decided on a pork brain, because canned ones are on supermarket shelves, so we mistakenly assumed meat markets would probably carry them. Not one store in three towns had an intact pig brain.

We were running out of time when I had one of those ah ha moments - Chesterfield had a meat packing plant with all kinds of animal parts. We arrived just as they were closing, only to be told they had no pork brains.

Aaron's disappointment was a tangible thing. I had let him down. Super Mom had dropped her cape. I was a failure. Right before we reached the door, the owner asked if it had to be a pork brain, said he had a cow head.

We yelled. We hugged. We were triumphant. The impossible was possible after all. Two dollars and fifty-cents was all it cost to restore my Super Mom status. I picked my cape up off the floor, put it back on and, with the cow head ensconced in a cardboard box, floated to the car.

"Mom, how are we going to get the brain out of the head?"

Such an innocent question, but so hard to answer. A cow has high bone density, and the brain is tightly wrapped in that heavy bone. I set it on the driveway and beat it with a hammer - not even a dent. I called my grown son Kevin. He might have better tools.

When I told him my predicament, I had to hold the phone away from my ear. His laughter was tinged with that same sarcastic disbelief I had been hearing all day, but I didn't have time to pursue it - I was desperate. Still laughing, he told me to bring it on up.

After driving twenty miles, I was unprepared for his shocked reaction when I opened the trunk. He didn't think I was serious. He had no idea how to extract a cow's brain from the head. I closed the trunk and headed back to Chesterfield.

I went to Daddy B who was always good at solving problems, but this one perplexed even him. It was too hard to smash with a mallet, but after studying it, Daddy B. sent his son for a saw. He sawed through the head, chips flying. We drove merrily away with our dislodged brain in the box.

Now we had to keep it fresh. Formaldehyde was not available to the public anymore, so I called a funeral home. When I asked the mortician if he could sell me enough formaldehyde to preserve a brain for a few days, he hung up on me.

I wasn't surprised at his rudeness because everyone I explained my problem to reacted similarly. I went in person to the next funeral home. This funeral director spoke a little sharply to me when refusing my request. I left empty-handed and a bit bewildered at his irritation.

We decided to try an old standard. We stopped by the store near our house and bought vinegar. I told the manager about our interesting search and everyone's strange reaction, and he burst into laughter.

"Jean", he said in between spurts of giggling, "Did you know today is April Fool's Day?"

God's Gift

When DeAnne was thirteen she would sometimes hang out with me at work. Much to the dismay of my co-workers and me, the owner had given his forty-five-ish daughter's thirty-ish boyfriend a job. Even though he had no qualifications whatsoever. He managed to constantly get in the way of those of us who were actually working.

Tall and thin, he wore his jeans so tight I don't know how he managed to breathe. This was before stretch jeans. And to use an old Southern term - the boy was full of himself. But the older ladies, including the boss's wife, loved him. Probably because he flirted shamelessly with them.

When DeAnne first met pretty boy, I watched her watching him and sighed. I just knew he was going to bowl her over like he had the older women.

I was wrong.

After observing him interact with the female customers for quite a bit, she leaned over and whispered. "Momma, why does he wear his jeans so tight?"

"Because someone told him he was God's gift to women," I

whispered back.

She looked at him again, then whispered, "Momma, somebody lied to him."

My Daughter.... Myself

My daughter was born after I had three sons. Although having a same gender child was an awesome thing, she was still a mysterious little package. It didn't take long to realize she had inherited my vivid imagination.

DeAnne was a mini-me, but even more fanciful than I had been as a child. The one area this was evident in was her play-acting. Many children pretend, but this precocious child developed roles that lasted for months.

It started with clothing. When she was three she would search her closet to find outfits to match her doll's clothing. At four she wore nothing but dresses for a year, no shorts or pants.

The summer she was five she wore swim suits from spring until fall. Even when I made her wear a dress to church, the swim suit would be under the dress, and she let me know she was not happy about that.

Then it progressed into role playing. I first noticed this one Sunday afternoon when we were dining out. The waitress commented on how pretty DeAnne was, followed by the predictable, "How old are you, sweetie?" DeAnne sat up straight like a miniature woman and, without batting an eyelash, said in her most courteous, adult voice, "Sixteen".

The waitress looked at me with an eyebrow lifted, a difficult thing to do. I have never mastered it. What a dilemma I was faced with. Should I be honest, or should I give my five-year-old the assurance that Mommy would always have her back.

I chose the child back option. "Yes", I said in *my* most courteous, adult voice, "She's sixteen." I felt like a fool, the waitress thought she had been bamboozled and DeAnne just sat there smiling.

I wasn't always so accommodating. Have you ever tried to read fabricated sign language from an eight-year-old pretending to be deaf? One day while trying to decipher which flavor of ice cream she wanted, I lost patience and told her to stop doing that finger thing.

DeAnne still didn't break character. She teared up. But she did it silently. I guess she figured adding sobs would blow her cover. Those huge blue eyes she used to manufacture her fake tears got to the cashier. He shot me a shame on you look and gave her the ice cream at no charge.

Once she pretended to be missing an arm. We were in a fast food place during this phase, and I sat silently watching as she unsuccessfully tried to open the plastic wrapped spoon with only one hand.

A man leaving with his take-out set his food down and smiled sadly at DeAnne. He opened the spoon for her, mumbled poor little thing and scowled at me as he retrieved his order from our table.

Sometimes the play acting worked to my advantage. When she was eleven I came home to a spotlessly clean kitchen floor. Even the cracks were free of dirt. As I stood staring in astonishment, she informed me she was pretending to be Cinderella and got carried away. My raggedy princess had cleaned the whole kitchen with a tiny scrub brush.

The pretense that caused the biggest confusion was what the family refers to as the twin thing. DeAnne convinced all of her school friends she had a twin sister named Dianne. Her older brother had photoshopped pictures to make it look as if she did have a twin. Although this had gone on for months, I was totally in the dark.

One day the mother of one of her classmates came to my workplace to tell me how sorry she was to hear of my daughter's car accident. I panicked and grabbed my purse, babbling out questions as we rushed to the front. When I asked if DeAnne was okay, the confused lady said not DeAnne, Dianne, her twin sister.

I guess uncontrolled laughter was not the expected reaction. Even after I explained, the other mother looked suspiciously askance at me, a look I had grown quite used to over the years. I hope she didn't judge my child rearing based on that one incident.

After the confused mother left, I called DeAnne and asked for an explanation in my stern Momma voice. She said she was tired of being a twin, and had decided to kill Dianne off. I was still laughing when I hung up the phone.

My little actress grew up. Along the way she played many parts and filled many roles, but always she entertained and amazed me. That vivid imagination was packed away with her Barbie dolls, and easy-bake oven. She graduated with high honors from USC and is as normal as a child of mine has a chance of being.

I raised four amazing children. They were and still are a joy. Over the years they have brought much laughter to my life. Their childhood and adult antics seem to be a reflection of my quirky view of life. Maybe it's a gene thing, or maybe it's simply a Jean thing.

Pumpkin Love

My dad, an old style Missionary Baptist preacher, didn't acknowledge many holidays. Halloween was just one of them. It wasn't that he objected to celebrating All Hallows Eve for religious reasons. For him it was a matter of pride. He could not bring himself to let his children ask strangers for candy.

Halloween was a non-event for me as a child. I never had a costume, never had a bag full of candy to rifle through. We lived in the country, so I never saw other kids dressed for Halloween either. No one ever knocked on our door asking for candy.

So, I didn't experience trick or treating until I was a parent. The first one was exciting for me. Especially since Tony was only one when I took him. That meant I got to eat most of the candy.

My four children were widely spaced and over the years the excitement waned. When DeAnne, my youngest, turned twelve, the cut-off age in our town, I breathed a sigh of relief. I had been trick or treating for twenty-seven years.

During those years I made homemade costumes, baked orange cakes with witches on them and attended a lot of Halloween parties. But I never decorated my house for Halloween. No stuffed witches on the lawn, no spider webs running through the house and no pumpkins on the porch.

In fact, I've only carved one pumpkin in my life, and it was three years after I quit celebrating Halloween.

My fifteen-year-old, DeAnne, had been hospitalized for over a month. Halloween was on the horizon, and, since she would be spending it in the hospital, I decided to carve her a pumpkin. This pumpkin needed to be really special, so I opted to make it look like a member of Korn, her favorite rock group.

Unfortunately, and kind of sad since I was in my forties, I had no experience in choosing pumpkins. I chose one that was not ripe enough for carving. But I didn't have any money to spare, so I was determined to carve this unripe pumpkin I had purchased. It took me over two hours to get the insides out.

Five hours, two bent spoons, a broken knife blade, one cut finger, and several skinned knuckles later, I placed the long, curly wig on the pumpkin head. The eyes weren't quite even, and the mouth was a little crooked, but I was too tired to care.

The next day I drove straight to the hospital from work, about a four-hour drive. I was still tired from the day before and dropped the pumpkin getting him out of the car. The split was almost covered by the wig, but there was a little gaping crevice beside his mouth, giving him a somewhat sinister look.

When I arrived at the check-in desk - it was a juvenile ward, so visitors had to be buzzed in - the lady said, "You'll have to leave the pumpkin here. We don't allow outside food on the ward." Deflated, defeated, almost in tears, I stood there holding my pitiful, broken pumpkin in both arms.

I wondered if this officiously cold lady knew how much of me was in that pumpkin, how much I missed my daughter, how useless I felt because I could do nothing for her except carve a stupid pumpkin, how sick she was, how sad I was. That's when something snapped.

I looked the lady squarely in the eye and said defiantly, "No!" Then I repeated it, "No!" She was a little taken aback at my fervor, but I paid no attention. I continued, "This pumpkin has no food in it. I know because I spent two hours scraping the insides out."

I shifted the pumpkin, stood a little taller and, with steel in my voice, said, "I am taking this pumpkin to my daughter. Call and get permission or buzz me in without it. I don't care."

My pumpkin and I headed toward the double doors. The lady told me to wait, she would call someone. The supervisor she called took the wig off, looked inside and told her to let me take the pumpkin in.

But the lady at the desk had to have the last word. After the supervisor left, she made me wait while she called security. Yes, my pumpkin and I were escorted into the ward by a guard who smiled at me when he deposited me at DeAnne's hospital room door.

Like I said, I've only carved one pumpkin in my life, but it was a doozy.

It's a Long, Long Ride

When my daughter DeAnne was fifteen she was being treated as an outpatient at The Medical University of Charleston. I rode up in the elevator with her every morning, handed her over to the nurse and went back to the motel until time to pick her up.

One morning I came down to find a local policeman standing beside my car writing a ticket. I asked him what the problem was, since the two-hour parking permit was clearly visible through my front window.

He informed me my car had been parked there longer than two hours. Forgetting I wasn't on my home turf, I told him it had only been there long enough for me to ride the elevator up and back down.

He stopped writing, looked over his glasses at me, and, in a stern voice, asked, "Ma'am, are you arguing with me?"

Remembering where I was, I quickly replied, "No sir, I was just commenting on what a long elevator ride that was."

He put his book away without finishing the ticket and told me in the future to stay within the two-hour limit. I resolved then and there to take a different elevator next time.

Fifty Dollar Sweatshirts

My son, Kevin, snapped a picture of me sitting at the end of a long pier on Kiawah Island. I'm so small you can barely see me. I was at a low point in my life when he took me there, and he knew it.

I felt like I had wandered into Lifestyles of the Rich and Famous. The lovely place we stayed in cost more a night than I made in a month. I winced every time Kevin paid for something because it was not cheap. He wouldn't even let me buy a soda.

At that time in my life I felt just like the figure in the photo - small and insignificant. My daughter had been extremely sick, in and out of hospitals, near death a couple of times, I had to sell all my things to move into a furnished house, my mom, my rock, was slowly moving into her own world leaving me behind, and the only thing I owned was a car.

I spent a lot of time sitting on that pier and walking on the beautiful beach, contemplating my life.

Before we left, Kevin insisted on buying me a souvenir sweatshirt. I stood beside the counter, unable to pick out one. The cheapest was $49.99. Kevin laughed at my reluctance, reached around me, picked up a sweatshirt and went to the cashier with it. I stood beside the counter there crying.

I came home, refreshed in mind and body, ready to fight another day. I hung the shirt in the back of my closet, unable to wear such an expensive thing for every day. DeAnne got better, life got better. The shirt hung there, reminding me of a time when a son's love gave me the strength to keep going.

One day, after it had hung in the closet for a couple of years, I pulled the sweatshirt out of the closet and wore it to the grocery store. For over a decade I wore it constantly, like a security blanket. I finally gave the now faded and stained shirt to Kevin, because I could not bring myself to throw it away.

Love comes in many forms, showing up right when you need it most. For me, the tiny figure sitting at the end of that pier, it came wrapped in a fifty-dollar sweatshirt.

Semantics

My daughter DeAnne was too small when her dad and I split up to notice my family's attitude toward divorce and dating. When I was first divorced, their attitude was total disapproval. But over the years they adjusted and eventually just treated me like the wild child in the family.

When DeAnne reached her teenage years, and especially when she had her own boyfriend, she picked up on the undercurrent of disapproval toward my lifestyle - that of a divorced, dating mom.

It was the fourth of July when she broached the subject with me. We had made a Nacho Belle Grande to celebrate the holiday. While we were sitting cross-legged on the floor eating she asked, "Momma, why does your family not like for you to date?"

I explained to her that it was more complicated than that. We were raised very strait-laced and mine was the first divorce in the family. They disapproved because we had been raised that divorce was wrong. That put dating after divorce completely outside the boundaries of what we had been taught.

She pondered that while she chewed, then said, "Momma, we're the family sluts, aren't we?"

White Horse

When I was a single mom, my favorite saying was, "Where's my white horse?" Shortening of a knight in shining armour on a white horse.

One afternoon DeAnne, who had just come home from another hospital stay, said, "Momma, I don't want to live like this anymore. Where's our white horse?" Then she burst into tears.

I shushed her and rocked her back and forth while she cried. After the sobbing stopped, she raised her head, looked at me and, as if she'd just realized it, said "Momma, you're our white horse."

I just smiled. I had known it all along.

I was driving down a country road with my now adult little girl this week when she yelled, "Momma, stop the car!" Alarmed, I pulled over on the side of the road. DeAnne jumped out of the car and ran up the hill.

She had seen a baby goat with his head caught in a wire fence. She untangled and freed him, despite his bucking the entire time. White horses aren't always horses. They come in all types of guises. Today it was a little skinny girl in blue jeans running up a hill.

A Girl and a Dog

When DeAnne was sixteen, we moved from Charleston to Pageland. The owner of the house we rented had moved into a nursing facility, but her dog, Frisco, still lived in the house. The family rented us the house on the condition we take care of Frisco.

I hadn't had a serious pet since I was a child, so I was a little apprehensive about moving into a house with a dog I knew nothing about. But DeAnne took to him right away, and he to her, although Frisco did not accept people easily,

He was a well-behaved dog – he never climbed on the furniture, didn't chew anything, seldom barked, and he never bothered any food left sitting around. However, he had many quirks, and a couple of phobias. It took us several months, but we eventually learned them all.

His most inexplicable phobia was his need to have doors open. None of the doors in the house caught when closed. I thought this may have been for Frisco's sake, because if we closed them, he would push them open with his nose.

We closed all the doors just to test our theory, and he nudged each door back open with his head. If he had trouble he would moan and scratch until we opened it for him. He would then lie down and play contentedly with his toys.

Our little unkempt dog would stand quietly for us to brush his fur, but at some point in the grooming - without warning - he would try to bite the hand that was brushing him. So, his grooming was a hit and miss affair.

He never allowed anyone to pat him on his head. He would growl and bare his teeth if we even reached our hand toward him. DeAnne was undaunted by his tough dog attitude. She would give him a quick pat and pull her hand away quickly, laughing. He allowed this, but only from DeAnne

It was as if he knew she wasn't well. DeAnne was suffering from a serious illness when we moved into Frisco's house, and he would lie quietly beside the bed or couch - wherever she happened to be.

When she was well enough to drive, he would listen for her car, barking as soon as he heard her turn down our street. When she entered the door, he was all over her, like a puppy in his excitement, and she was as glad to see him. Frisco received her first greeting...always.

DeAnne developed a fierce loyalty to her adopted pet. We took him for his regular trim one day, and when we picked him up he was in a cage, trembling. DeAnne told the groomer what she thought of that, and Frisco was never allowed to get a professional trim again.

So, I purchased pet clippers, and we attempted the job ourselves. Imagine trying to clip a dog that doesn't allow you to touch his head, and without any provocation will suddenly reach back and try to bite you. He had short hair, long hair, and almost no hair, but it was all done with love by his adoring, adopted mistress.

One afternoon DeAnne called me at work in a state of panic. A pit bull was attacking Frisco. I told her to call the police since we lived right around the corner from them.

When I pulled in my driveway the owner of the other dog, a policewoman, and DeAnne were all freaking out. The dogs were soaking wet because DeAnne had hosed them down.

As I climbed from my car DeAnne was screaming," Shoot him! Shoot him!

The policewoman yelled back, "I can't shoot him! I've never shot a dog!"

DeAnne cried, "Then give me your gun! I'll shoot him!"

This spurred the owner to action, and she pulled her dog off Frisco, who suffered a torn ear and a couple of cuts, but nothing major, thanks to his fierce protector.

Frisco was old when he came into our lives, so after only a few years with us, he became so ill, the vet could not heal him. We knew it was the end but could not find it within us to have him put to sleep. The love of this precious animal had seen DeAnne through the worst illness of her life.

He had also lain beside her bed while she grieved over her Dad's passing. She had loved that frowsy-haired dog when she didn't have the strength to love anything or anyone else. Frisco appreciated the gift she gave him and had loved her in return, allowing her liberties he gave no one else.

During his last illness, she slept on the couch with him beside her on the floor, too sick to move. Even in his sickness, he wouldn't climb on the furniture. But, on the last night of his life Frisco left DeAnne sleeping on the couch and managed to pull himself into her bedroom to die.

It was a faithful pet's final act of love for the girl he had cherished.

Who Is You?

I have always been a tolerant person myself, but when my husband and I separated after twenty-two years of marriage and four children, his girlfriend put a big strain on my tolerance level. Completely understandable because they had started dating a couple of years before we separated.

After they moved in together she tried to draw me into their relationship by sending me presents. She sent me tube socks for my birthday, a photo album for Christmas, and even sent me an Easter corsage. When he came to pick up the kids on the weekend, she would send me things like boxes of doughnuts. Well half a box of doughnuts. She split them with me.

My husband - this was before the divorce, so he was still my husband - begged me to humor her. "Jean, just give her a chance," he pleaded. "She will be your best friend if you let her."

I declined his offer, but then had to explain specifically why this wasn't going to happen any time soon. Why am I always the only realist in the group?

Over the years I managed to maintain a cordial but distant relationship with the two of them. We came together for family events such as my youngest son's graduation and my daughter's sixteenth birthday, but our interaction was minimal.

Still, she kept trying to find a place for me. I have no idea why. Guilt perhaps. This continued for at least ten years after the divorce. At my oldest son's thirtieth birthday party, she introduced me to her brother.

As I was shaking his hand, she said cheerfully, "This is the one we want to fix you up with. I gave her my you-can't-be-serious look, but she didn't notice. She thought she had finally found a way to have me in their lives.

I shook his hand, told him he was probably a nice guy, but that would be a little too weird for me. The family connections were confusing enough for ex-husband's four-year-old son without me dating his uncle.

There's a picture of me from that party holding their little boy in my lap. I have my head thrown back laughing. He's looking up at me. He had stepped on a sandspur, and I distracted him while my son, his big brother, jerked it out.

Dirty tears streaking his face, he had asked, "Who is you anyway?"

Journalist to the Stars

My son, Kevin, lives in Matthews, North Carolina, but he called me a couple of months ago to inform me he will be co-starring in *Love Letters*, a play being performed at the Creative Spot in Ruby, South Carolina.

Kevin is an extremely talented, young-ish man. He's a brilliant writer, cartoonist, and conversationalist, but he has never spoken or performed in front of a group. He even managed to make it through speech class in college without actually speaking.

Co-star, Charity Rollins, on the other hand, is a gifted actress and director. Theater was her major in college, and she has even acted in this particular play before. Life interrupted her dream, as it tends to do sometimes, but four babies later she's picked up that dream, dusted it off, and is running with it.

So why did she offer an ingénue like Kevin a starring role in her first major production? There are no bit parts, no walk-ons, and, hopefully, no walk-offs or walk-outs when my boy looks out at the people who paid ten dollars to see him do his thing, and he forgets what his thing is.

I allowed my imagination free reign trying to surmise the reasons behind this oddly crooked detour on Kevin's road to adulthood. Yes, he's thirty-eight. It takes some of us longer.

I finally decided my son, who is getting long in the tooth, has a bucket list and acting was on it. Charity and Kevin's girlfriend, are friends, so I assumed she pulled some strings to get him the part.

"Not so," says Charity, "It was a no-brainer. Kevin has a huge personality and he loves to play. We're roughly the same age, we interact in a way that makes people laugh, we both really love goats, and he was drunk when I asked him to do it. I took advantage of the situation and make no apologies for it."

Trying to examine this the way a professional journalist would, I asked Kevin what his motivation was. He replied with a very straight face, "Fear of upsetting Charity".

Charity agrees that he is quite scared of her. Apparently wearing the same clothes to six weeks of rehearsal caused the feisty director to put this fear in him early on.

Although he's still wearing the clothes, Kevin says he will draw on that and other experiences with Charity to make his role more convincing. According to him the woman in the play is an attention craving, crabby, selfish slut.

A look from Charity stopped him before he could elaborate

further. In rebuttal Charity stated she had to teach him everything except how to read.

While most of the conflict between these two delightful personalities has been resolved amicably, Charity says Kevin's lackadaisical attitude toward promptness and his stage fright continue to be a problem.

Kevin countered with the fact he was willing to drive through 77 stop lights, around 32 curves, pass 4 tractors, dodge golf carts and four wheelers - after crossing the state line - and navigate through Ruby just to be the ivory statue to her Pygmalion.

As for the stage fright, Kevin assures us he is just afraid he will be unable to concentrate when people in the audience hold up placards with his name on them and start throwing their underwear on stage. Charity dismisses this explanation and has asked me to confiscate Kevin's passport to ensure he won't leave the country before opening night.

Kevin insists he is not a diamond in the rough, but a thoroughly polished, sensitive Renaissance man who can rip Sam Elliot's mustache off and make a lovely flower out of it, whose celebrity status on Facebook will be a big draw-in.

Charity accused me of throwing that in because I'm his mom and refuses to defer to him as a celebrity. It is quite obvious Charity and Kevin, much like the characters they play, bring different viewpoints and life experiences to *Love Letters*. Their energetic and charismatic interaction with each other in real life has to be a plus for the audience.

So apparently Ruby is the new Hollywood and Kevin a modern-day James Dean, good- looking and full of angst, but with less hair and acting ability.

The road to Hollywood is paved with bad auditions, and Charity is a brave woman. Although, figuratively speaking, the two drive in separate vehicles, hopefully for the audience they will arrive at the same destination.

Love Letters is a play which spans fifty years of communication between a woman and man and portrays the ins and outs of relationships. It is intended for mature audiences, but neither one of the stars will say if nudity is involved.

I need to know before I buy my ticket. This is my son, after all. As for Kevin, Charity says if he gets his act together – pun intended - she may not charge him admission.

Good to Go

I was raised to be dependent on my husband and spent a lot of years this way. DeAnne was my only daughter, so I raised her to never depend on a man financially. In fact, to be independent in all areas of her life.

About the time DeAnne started driving, I had a friend who was injured by an exploding battery. I decided it was time to make sure my baby girl could tell the positive from the negative on a set of battery cables. I used word association to teach her, something I did quite often with all my children. It's the writer in me.

The last time we were at the gym together I ran my battery down. We needed a jump. DeAnne went back inside the gym and found a nice young man to help us. While he was connecting the cables on his jeep, she connected the cables on our car, surprising the young man as well as me.

It was a pleasant surprise, though, because, after almost twenty years, she had not forgotten. "You remembered," I told her with a smile.

"How could I forget?" she answered. "Red stands for red-light house. A red-light house is full of prostitutes. Prostitutes starts with a P. Positive starts with a P."

While I may have winced a little at my unconventional teaching method, I kept smiling. Because unconventional or not my system WORKED!

However, for a mother raised the way I was, some things aren't so easy to teach. When DeAnne started dating, I wasn't as comfortable with the birds and bees talk as I would have liked to be. I'm afraid I probably left out a few of the more important ones.

When DeAnne became single again after six years of being out of the dating scene, I decided it would be a good time to fill in the parts I missed. Although it was a little late in the game for the obligatory mother daughter birds and bees talk with her, I felt like I had a lot to offer in the area of dating after divorce.

I began our conversation by cautioning her that having a physical relationship with someone you don't care about can be an unfulfilling experience, something many single women still haven't learned.

She responded with, "I know, mom. I've been married."

It was an extremely short mother daughter talk, but I knew she was good to go.

Follow the Bouncing Ball

I have a mast cell condition which causes me to have allergic reactions to just about everything. After almost a year of not being able to breathe well, passing out from not being able to breathe well, and frequent lung infections, I was diagnosed with additive allergies and asthma.

It was years before the mast cell problem was recognized as the actual culprit and what had looked like separate problems were found to have a connection.

Meanwhile I spent a lot of time in the offices of various specialist, getting misdiagnosed constantly, then having to deal with the original problem as well as reactions to the treatment. That's why I wasn't too concerned when I was diagnosed with a brain tumor.

I went to the doctor because I had been experiencing constant dizziness for about six weeks. It was a new nurse-practitioner who told me I had a brain tumor. All I did was walk a line and stand on one foot, and she made this split-second diagnosis. I was sent home on complete bed rest, to await a brain scan.

My four children came, from one place or another, and decided to take my mind off the problem by taking me shopping. I wasn't as worried as they were, because I knew there was nothing growing in my brain.

After several misdiagnoses, I had learned to be skeptical of these pronunciations, but the kids wanted to be with me in my hour of confusion.

The doctor had ordered bed rest and no driving, so the kids plopped me in a wheel chair to take me around Walmart. Then they started arguing over who was going to push me. While Tony, Aaron and DeAnne were arguing, Kevin just took off with me.

The other three started chasing us. So, there I was flying through Walmart in a wheel chair, taking corners on two wheels. As I held on for dear life, I was thinking this isn't exactly what the nurse-practitioner had in mind.

I was so relieved when my daughter finally got control of the wheel chair. But then her brother Tony tried to grab me from her. She feinted and ran to the side. I was now the basketball in a two-man game.

As I was being shunted back and forth, I knew without a doubt I did not have a brain tumor. Because this would have shaken it loose for sure.

The Spirit of Christmas

Doug and I went shopping for some household items, and I saw people filling the trunks of their older model cars with toys, electronics, and quite a few big-ticket items. I wondered if it was a wise thing to do in today's economy, this Christmas craziness of throwing financial caution to the wind.

Did shopping mania really embody the Christmas spirit? I decided to write a column on overspending during the holidays. My attitude would have been worthy of old Scrooge himself. However, half-way in I had a change of heart. It is Christmas, after all, and not the time for a bah humbug kind of article.

Doug went to bed and left me with my thoughts. The house was quiet. I ran through mental photos from Christmases past. They are probably similar to those of most people in my age bracket.

Real cedar trees shedding nettles in the living room, stockings made out of daddy's socks, waking to a cold house in the wee hours of the morning, firecrackers, sparklers, parades, Christmas plays at church, food, lots of food, and presents, always presents.

More memorable than the presents themselves are the smiles they evoked from my parents, brother, sister, and, of course, me. Christmas was a happy oasis in an often times harsh world, a respite from the rigidness of our everyday lives.

Long after we were too old for Santa, my mom still bought us gifts. I was her designated gift wrapper. She let me see my own gift, then made me wrap it, so I could open it with the rest of the family.

Even when the great-grandchildren started coming, Miss Hallie still bought each one of us a gift. In addition to my present, she bought me a jacket every year, but in a style and color she liked.

I would wait a year or two, then give the jacket back to her. I told her I was cleaning out my closet and found something I thought she would like. It was my own version of re-gifting.

The year she lost two sisters, she went overboard. She bought the boys a television, and the girls a piano.... on credit, I'm sure. I felt so guilty, but she was making a statement in her own way.

Closing the door on Christmas past, I went to bed. The column would have to wait. The Christmas holidays had brought with them a special kind of writer's block.

The next day, I went with my daughter to pick up a Christmas gift she had ordered for a friend. FedEx had left the two packages in the office of her apartment complex, and she was sure they would fit in my car.

She had found a company that made photos into paintings and was so eager to see how they looked she opened one of them on the sidewalk outside of the office. The happiness on her face when she saw how well they turned out was contagious, and I smiled with her.

I told her she should wait to open the larger package. She reluctantly consented and started putting the smaller one back in the box. I headed to my car with the large one. Oh dear, it wouldn't fit in the car.

I gave her the bad news, but it didn't dim her smile. She picked up the five-foot long box, perched it at a rather precarious angle against her shoulder and head and took off walking.

Her apartment was at the opposite end of the large complex. Shaking my head at the exuberance of youth, I picked up the painting she had repackaged and put it in the car. I was glad that one fit, because I was way too old to hoist it on my head.

Since she works fulltime and goes to college fulltime, I was almost certain she had put the gifts on her credit card. Of course, I didn't ask. She pays her own bills, and it wasn't my business.

I remembered doing the same thing when I was a young parent. We couldn't always stretch our budget to handle items like Eviel Kneivel bicycles.

When that happened, we went down to Hurst Western Auto where Jeep, Cheryl, Frankie, or Julious would let us sign on the dotted line and help us load the toys into our - yep - older model car. Christmas bought on credit was worth those monthly payments when our children saw their gifts on Christmas Day.

I could almost feel Scrooge scowling at my change in attitude, as I watched this skinny woman-child carrying a package larger than she was down the street. She had made me realize Christmas is not about the receiver - it's about the giver.

It's the one time of year we allow ourselves to splurge on those we love, to enjoy a day of indulgence unlike any other. Blowing the budget once a year isn't going to break us, and the sacrifice is worth the reward.

As I passed DeAnne holding that big package against her head, she smiled at me, and I realized I had just glimpsed the Spirit of Christmas present walking down the street. I think I felt Scrooge wince.

Home is...

I made no New Year's resolutions for 2012. I know this sets me apart from the rest of America, just as not eating black-eyed peas and collard greens on New Year's Day sets me apart from most Southerners.

My thoughts were quite complex as this year started. Miss Hallie, my vivacious little mother, passed away in September, and I knew I had to face 2012 without her in it. Because of this, the New Year found me pondering my mother's life and how it is reflected in mine. This, in turn, led me to wonder how my life has affected my own children.

When I look in the mirror these days, I see very little of the girl I once was. This is to be expected. Time and experience changes us all, physically as well as mentally and spiritually. We have no control over it. Change is a natural process.

Becoming the woman I am now was not an easy crossing. I, like the fabled cat, have lived several lives since my first one which played out in Chesterfield, a small, friendly town in South Carolina.

That first life was important, not just for the indelible impression it left on my mind and psyche, but for the core values I acquired during the living of it. I was part of a family for sixteen years. We prayed together, before meals and at bedtime.

We sang together, at home and in church. We argued over the bathroom and which television shows to watch. We got upset with and forgave each other...often. Through it all we were a family. We had a place we belonged.

I would like to say my mother encouraged me to be my own person, but that was unheard of in her generation. Instead she had a two-part goal in mind for her three children – graduate from high school and find a good husband or wife.

The things parents of today worry about, drinking, gambling, drugs, weren't even on Miss Hallie's radar. She firmly believed her children would never do any of those things. And we didn't.

From watching my mother, I learned to adapt without complaint to the situations life dropped me into. I wonder if she knew this would be the most valuable tool she handed me.

Emulating my Mom's approach to the changes in her own life helped me tremendously when I married at sixteen. I had lived in the same house my entire life, but Tony was born a rambling man, and ramble we did.

We never lived anywhere long enough to grow roots. By the time Tony, Jr. and Kevin were teenagers we had moved twenty times. When my husband met the love of his life, the kids and I moved on alone. On my own after twenty two years, permanency still eluded me.

As I thought about the things I learned from watching my Mom, I wondered what my children had learned from watching me. A single mother has a hard time competing with two parent homes. To have enough money you have to give up time. To have time, you have to give up money. And there's never enough energy. It is an inescapable circle.

Tony, Jr. married and left before the divorce, then Kevin. Aaron left for college, the navy, and California in that order. And, finally, DeAnne married and moved away. Thoughts of my Mom turned into thoughts of me as a mom. Did my love and concern for my children show through all the changes in our lives?

Wondering about these things interfered with my sleep. I put on my robe and sat in the living room. To escape my thoughts I turned on the computer. I was still logged onto Facebook. The first thing I saw was a posting by my son, Kevin. It was a Beatles video, "Do You Want to Know a Secret?" Above it he had written:

"I remember my mom singing this song, rocking me back and

forth in the rocking chair a few feet away from the front door to Granny's house on Green Street in Chesterfield. I can feel her hands on my back as I look over at the door. I can feel the comfort in her voice as she tells me she loves me. The song is intimate. The song is powerfully intimate, even in the disguise of bubblegum. I'm 40 now...mom is more than that...but I can remember a time when we were both innocent and young and a rocking chair on Green Street was all the home in the world."

The answer to my searching was in my son's post on Facebook. Home is not a building made of wood or brick. It can't be seen with the eyes. It is felt with the heart. No matter where we are geographically, Tony, Kevin, Aaron, DeAnne, and I are a family. We will always have a place we belong.

The House That Jack Built

My daddy and my Uncle Jack built the house I grew up in. It was a simple four room A-frame house, no halls, no bathroom and no running water (that didn't come until I was thirteen). We did have electricity - walking in high cotton we were. The front porch had a sloping roof so close to the ground, we kids used to jump off of it for fun.

There was also a full screened-in back porch where we took baths in tin wash tubs when the weather was warm. My mom did her canning out there as well as her clothes washing. In a ringer washing machine with a hose stuck out the door to drain the water.

At some point the men in the family and a couple of neighbors made half of that porch into a bedroom. We took turns claiming it. This is where, my imagination flourished, where I started writing as soon as I could hold a pencil.

I also read probably thousands of books under that tin roof - I am convinced to be a writer, you must first be a reader - whether it was my turn to claim the room or not. There was no personal space back then.

The old house was demolished years ago, after standing empty for decades. For my birthday one year, my oldest son, Tony, went to the site, gathered up some broken bits of the house that built me and made them into a bird house.

A piece of that old tin roof where Jean, the writer, came into being covers his creation. He reached into the rubble, captured a memory and brought it to life with his talented hands. So, my then house is here in my now house.

Somehow it seems like the pieces of all that I am have been seamed together with the melding of these two houses. While I am deeply grateful for where I am now, I am as equally grateful for where I came from. It laid the foundation for who I am today. Thank you again, Tony Smith, for this unique, unmatchable gift.

Burned in the Fire

When my son Kevin was small, he was entranced with what I called my memory box. It was a cardboard box that held my notebook full of poems and magazines with my published poems in them.

On the same shelf were bunches of high school yearbooks from across the United States that had, with Teen Magazine's permission, used one of my poems as their theme. But he was especially taken with my venture into fiction, a short story called Henry. He read and reread it so much he knew it by heart.

I also wrote columns for three local papers when he was a child. This didn't qualify me as a syndicated columnist. They were small papers. The poems, magazines, yearbooks, and copies of my columns were lost in a fire that destroyed our home.

Losing all my writings affected me deeply. I reacted by laying my pen down.

I stopped writing.

From the time he got his first job, Kevin started giving me writing paraphernalia as gifts. These segued from composition books and ink pens to a word processor, then a computer. The boy was determined I should write. Every gift came with a, "Momma, you need to write again."

Finally, I did. Once again, I became a newspaper columnist, and the writing gifts stopped. He had accomplished his goal. Momma was writing again.

Then, in 2011, he delved into his childhood memories, pulled that short story called Henry out of the fire and wrote a play based on it. Drama Mama Studios, a little theater group in South Carolina, performed it. I was a VIP guest, honored as the original writer.

I sat in a chair reserved just for me and watched characters I thought were gone forever, burned in the fire, come to life and walk around on stage. When he asked for another story, I gave him one called "Sunlight and Shadows". He gave it back to me, said it was a book.

He was right. "Sunlight and Shadows" became my first book. But it lay on the closet shelf for two years. Until my youngest, son, Aaron, told me I was too good a writer to not be read. He took my book, designed a cover photo for it, got it published, put it on Amazon, and built a website to sell it from.

It's a good feeling when your children make you proud. But it's an even greater feeling when you make your children proud.

Sweet Southern Woman

Sweet Southern Woman

My husband Doug was reading in bed. I went in and lay down across from him. He put his book down and waited patiently for me to speak. I never interrupt him when he's reading, so he knew it was important. With a sigh I asked, "What am I like. How do other people see me?"

"Well," he said, after a pause. "You're the most hard-headed woman I've ever met, but smart, really smart."

"What about sweet?" I asked. "People say I'm sweet."

He took off his glasses, probably to protect them, before answering. Struggling to phrase it properly, he finally threw in the towel and said, "Let's face it, darling. Neither one of us is sweet."

He waited apprehensively for my reaction and seemed relieved when I laughed and said, "I know. I've been trying to tell them that."

No, I'm not sweet, but I used to be. I was raised by my parents to be the typical old-fashioned Southern woman, and I was a dutiful daughter. Nothing was expected of me except to marry a good provider, have his children, and spend the rest of my life saying, "Yes, dear".

The transition from dutiful daughter to dutiful wife was an easy one. For twenty years I was a den mother, grade mother and Sunday school teacher. I baked cookies almost every day.

I learned to squelch the rational, thinking part of me and immersed myself in the day to day affairs of running a household. The term married with children could have been invented for me.

I had dinner on the table every evening when my husband walked in the door. I stayed within the parameters of my weekly grocery allowance, was a good mother to our four children, and forgave my mate every few years when I caught him en flagrante with his latest girlfriend.

But I was watching...and learning. The "Yes, dears" were getting harder to maintain.

You see, for a long time I believed the clichés I was raised on - the husband is the head of the household, pretty is as pretty does, a woman's place is in the home. But underneath that plastic exterior that had been molded to conform to my family and society's moors, there was something stirring.

I can't pinpoint a particular time in the marriage when I realized I was more intelligent, more realistic and, sadly, more ethical than my dreamer husband, but I knew. Yet, he made all the decisions in our home. I was more financially savvy than he was, but his was the only name on the checkbook.

It wasn't easy admitting to myself, much less anyone else, that what other people saw as the perfect family was nothing more than a hypocrisy. This hypocrisy went unexposed, because we were both taught what happens in the home stays in the home.

So, my coming of age was an extremely slow process.

Until one day my husband came home with balloons and a birthday cake.

When I asked who they were from, he mouthed the name that had, most recently, been coupled with his all over town. I had refused to give credence to the rumors, but the truth was there in the air between us.

My unrepentant husband filled our daughter's room with the helium balloons and deposited the cake on the bar. The next day, while he was at work, I went into my three-year-old's room armed with a safety pin and busted the balloons.

Crawling around on the floor, I painstakingly picked up every tiny piece out of the carpet, crying as I crawled. Because I knew my marriage was as broken as the balloons. Drying my eyes with the back of my hand, I threw the balloon remnants in the trash and headed for the cake.

It was a Peter Paul Mound cake, lavishly decorated. If not for their feverish movement, I wouldn't have noticed all the tiny sugar ants. They had found his cake. I watched them for a few minutes before deciding on a course of action.

Smiling, I picked up the now ant-decorated cake and put it in the freezer, leaving it in there long enough to freeze the little foragers. Over the next few days I kept the kids away from it and felt the weight of generations of sweet Southern women slipping from me every time my husband ate a piece.

We divorced not long after that. Although of long duration, our marriage was shallow. We eventually stopped trying to place blame and went on with our separate lives, both relieved the charade was over.

My husband never knew I fed him ants. Unlike Lot's wife, I never looked back. Freed from being that sweet Southern woman, I wake each day to the happiness of being just me.

For several years I didn't tell anyone what I had done, but one day I shared the story with my boss. After my confession, every so often he would say, "Are we good Jean? You aren't mad at me about anything are you?"

If my answer was no, he would ask me to get him a cup of coffee. I would smile and do as he asked but inside, from the ashes of another life, that sweet Southern woman was pounding the air with her fist and saying, "Yes!"

Moving On

I was raised in a Baptist family that did not acknowledge divorce. They had a "you made your bed, you have to lie in it" attitude toward marriage. So, I held on... twenty years longer than I should have, suffering through each new affair, year after year.

Then my husband's lies caught up with him. Circumstances forced him to confess he had fallen in love with a Waffle House (or Huddle House - details blur) waitress while at the same time telling me he wanted to keep HIS family, because he liked having a family....and a girlfriend.

Then the man I had been married to for twenty-two years left for work, unconcerned by, perhaps even unaware of the emotional havoc he had just caused. When he left, I screamed my mantra of twenty years to the walls of my empty house, to a God I had been told wouldn't listen.

"Please make him love me. Please make him love me," I begged crying. Standing there, defeated, deflated, in the grip of a twenty-year sadness.

Then I heard a voice say clearly, distinctly, kindly, "Loose him and let him go."

That was the beginning of my doing what I had to do, letting go of my husband, my marriage my life. I got a divorce, the only one ever in my family of five children, rented a tiny house four towns over, and bought a Country Squire Station Wagon for $125.

Then my children and I went on alone, and in the process, I learned a big lesson - that often times man is more rigid than God.

My Greatest Weakness

I was a studious child and immersed myself in books as soon as I could sound out words. Reading material was scarce at our house, so I would devour any kind of books I happened upon. I read my father's Zane Grey paperbacks, my mother's true crime magazines, and my big sister's true confession ones. I even read a whole set of Bible Encyclopedias when I was nine.

Though I had an extreme thirst for knowledge, attending college was an unattainable goal for me. My father considered any form of higher education for females a waste of money. He believed a woman's role in life was to marry and have children.

Limited by my raising, I did just that. For twenty-two years I was a stay-at-home wife and mother. Until my husband confessed he had met the love of his life in a Waffle House restaurant. Standing on my un-mowed lawn watching the dust settle behind his gold Monte Carlo, I wished my father had offered his daughters more than one option.

Living in the limbo land between separation and divorce was a sink or swim situation. There was nothing to do except take a deep breath and jump in. My first major obstacle was finding a job. Job hunting was a very traumatic experience.

After being rejected by the center of my universe, mustering the courage to face more rejection was a daily hurdle. With only a high school diploma, and no job experience, I seldom made it to the interview stage.

Finally, I snagged an interview for story-teller at the county library. Though lacking in experience, I was sure I would be hired. As the mother of four, I had told countless bedtime stories, often making them up as I went along.

I went into the interview with confidence. I was comfortable with the questions, I was articulate and, when the interviewer asked if I had been published, I was able to reply yes. This made my confidence level rise even higher.

Still, I was losing steam. This was only my second job interview, and it had gone into overtime. I had been job–hunting, without results, for weeks. As the interview was coming to an end, I braced myself for the last question. I was almost home free.

Then the interviewer asked me to name my greatest weakness.

I replayed that question many times over the next few days and came up with some great answers. But at the time it was asked, I was a depressed, desperately-needing-a-job mother with children to feed. The stress caused my brain to freeze.

I stared blankly at the man for several tension-filled seconds before mentally admitting defeat. Sighing, I replied quietly, sadly, "I can't think of any."

I am sure the interviewer was not impressed with my lack of humility. I didn't get the job. I finally found a full-time and a part-time job. I didn't like one and hated the other, but liking my job was not a luxury I could afford. I still lived in a two-income household, and now I had to provide both incomes.

Working two jobs didn't leave much time for just plain relaxing, but as the children grew older, Wednesday afternoons were my down time. DeAnne and I would go to Grits and Groceries, buy two pints of ice cream – Butter Pecan for her and Cherry Vanilla for me – and watch the television show *Charmed*.

One Wednesday night we sat down with our ice cream and propped our feet on the coffee table, only to discover our favorite program had been moved to Thursday nights. Disappointed, we turned the TV off and sat there talking.

DeAnne, who was thirteen, said, "Mom, it's kind of sad, isn't it? My life is just beginning and yours is almost over." Such wisdom from one so young. I reached over, confiscated her ice cream, and finished it off.

Almost twenty years have passed since that day I watched my husband drive away to be with the woman he loved. I fulfilled my responsibilities to my children, waiting until the last one graduated from college to obtain my own college degree.

Contrary to what my father believed, females do need an education. Acquiring one assuaged a life-long yearning. However, that twenty-year journey I took with my children through the ins and outs of life was much more educational than the schooling I received from the institution of higher learning.

And DeAnne, my little punkin' head, you were wrong. My life, too, had just begun.

There Ain't Nothing Wrong with The Radio

The headlight on my daughter's car kept burning out. After three visits to the dealership, they found the problem... using a computer of course. More and more I am realizing cars just aren't any fun anymore. I grew up in the days of shade-tree mechanics. Repairing each other's cars was a family past time.

Most of the men in my family could throw a rope over a tree limb, pull the motor out and rebuild it if need be. Sometimes one of the guys in the group, which included brothers, fathers, sons, uncles, cousins, husbands of cousins, and best friends of cousins, would even have a permanent pulley hanging on a limb.

The car I drive now doesn't even squeak. We had a rattle last week, drove my husband Doug bananas. It was my glasses laying in the glove compartment inset. I didn't tell him right away. It was too much fun watching him try to find it.

Finally, I showed him, then laughed at him for letting a little rattle rattle him. I have fond memories of bouncing down the road with so many things rattling it would have been impossible to pinpoint one specific source.

I don't think my first husband Tony and I ever had a car without mechanical problems. We drove them anyway. He hated car payments and had a knack for finding cheap cars. Our first car was a Ford that cut off the minute it stopped moving. We couldn't crank it again until it had sat for an hour or so.

After church one Sunday night my mom and I wanted a soda. Tony drove very slowly by the door of the little country store near our church, and my mom jumped out. Leaving the door open, he circled the gas pumps, drove back by the store.

With only a slight hesitation, because if you don't move you lose, I followed her. Several circles later we had jumped back into the open door of the still moving car holding our sodas. Pepsi addicts need their fix, even at the risk of life or limb.

Over the course of a lifetime I have owned every lemon that was manufactured. I know this because Doug told me. He laughed when I was recalling some of the cars I had bought. When I got to the Chevy Vega, he just shook his head.

I really loved that little hatchback with the gearshift between the seats, but Dixie, my husband's Doberman, didn't. She was the last thing we transported when we moved from Chesterfield to Pageland. Dixie was long and leggy, so her loving owner left the hatchback up, to give her enough room.

When Tony shifted gears crossing the highway I heard a loud thump. Looking back, I saw Dixie rolling down the road. Frantically I yelled, "Stop!"

He pulled the car over, and we jumped out. Dixie was on her feet by then. She saw us running toward her and took off running in a different direction, determined to not get back in that car. I let Tony chase her. I was not going to get near that unhappy Doberman.

I have driven a car without a heater, a car without brakes, a car without a window, a car with only two lug nuts on one wheel, a car without a rear-view mirror, a car without windshield wipers, a car without a door handle, and even a car without an ignition. Yep, no ignition. I loved them all. Having my own car has always represented freedom to me.

I have even owned a Starfire. Never heard of that one, have you?

Neither had the courthouse when I went to pay taxes on it. They had to make me up a tax to charge me. It was in someone's barn when I found it. It met my only criteria - it cranked.

After I cleaned all the hay out of it, I learned my little Starfire had all kinds of issues. The one that bothered me the most was the paint job. There wasn't one. It had been sprayed with primer, but never painted. I had four children and couldn't afford the paint, so I drove it anyway.

One day, not long after I bought it, my manager asked if she could use my car to go to the bank. I asked if she knew how to drive a four in the floor. She assured me she did, so I reached in my pocket for the keys.

"Just a couple of things," I told her, holding the keys out. "The key won't work if you put it all the way in. You have to pull it back out just a tad before it will turn."

She reached her hand out for the keys. As I handed them to her, I said, "And you need to pump the gas three times before you turn the key, not two, not four, three times exactly."

She took the keys and started toward the door. "Oh yeah," I added.

"Don't leave it running, because it will jump into reverse from neutral. Pump the brakes four times before you use them, not three, not five, four exactly. Put the emergency brake on when you park, because sometimes it jumps into reverse from park, too."

She stopped, turned around, and handed me the keys. "I've decided to walk to the bank," she said with an edge to her voice.

Some people just don't have a sense of adventure.

Lessons Learned – Lessons Shared

I married the first boy I dated in high school. I was sixteen. When we divorced twenty-two years later, the only relationship I knew how to have with a man was that of wife. The first time I was asked out after the divorce, I panicked.

This stranger wanted my home address and phone number. That thought was scary enough. However, when I thought about greeting him at my front door and climbing into his car, I began an investigation worthy of Scotland Yard.

This is so easy to accomplish in a small Southern town and is totally acceptable behavior in most parts of the South. You always know someone who knows someone who knows him.

By the end of my interrogation, I knew his job title, what kind of car he drove, the ex-wife's name, who his parents were, what school he attended, and when he graduated. Eureka, he graduated with my niece.

I called Roni, and she vouched for him. So, twenty years after graduation my criteria for going out with a man - he was valedictorian of his class. I gave him my address, made the date and left town that weekend, thus avoiding the issue altogether.

I have learned a few things since that first disastrous attempt. Let me share these with you, my sisters out there on the front line or still lying low in the trenches dodging bullets.

First, forget any advice Doctor Phil ever gave on dating. It doesn't apply to us. My grandson could find men for those lovely, articulate, young women he brings on his show. Oh, let's be truthful – my grandson is probably old enough to date some of those women. Doctor Phil needs to challenge himself. He should try to find me a date.

Secondly, don't be too proud to ask around. Trust your friends. Rumors may not be true, but they are usually based in fact. If your best friend hears his name and can't keep the look of astonishment off her face, you might want to turn that date down.

Another thing I learned is stay within your decade when dating younger men. If all you hear when he plays his music is the thump of the base, he's probably too young. If in doubt, don't hesitate to check ID. Even though cougar-ing up is acceptable, do you really want to date someone who went to school with your kids?

While we're on that subject, never, no matter how tempting, lie about your age in a small town. Ladies, we attended elementary school with many of the single men in this dating pool. They know our hair should really be gray. They may remember our natural color, even if we have forgotten.

Also, if possible, avoid the fixer uppers. Yes, there are men out there who, like a starter house, need work. This was my hobby for many years. I would crawl around hammer in hand, nails in mouth trying to patch up their rotten spots. I eventually learned there was more damage than I had nails for and hung up my tool belt.

This one is important. I will type slowly so you get the full effect. You will regret it if you let your friends set you up. This NEVER works. I think the worst set-me-up experience I had was my ex-husband's new wife deciding I was perfect for her brother. Try explaining that one to the grandkids.

I am now going to give you some very liberating advice - your date is not your husband. You don't have to refill his tea, light his cigarette, massage his feet, watch television programs you don't like, or babysit his dog. Just say no.

Finally, the most valuable lesson I have learned is you do not have to marry every man you date. While it is certainly flattering to have a man crazy over you three months in, it is also premature. Squash that sweet Southern raising. Throw politeness out the window in this situation.

As for me I am still waiting for my dream man to take me by the hand and whisper all those wonderful things I have been waiting to hear - Baby, I really love your kids. Don't worry about my new truck, it's just a scratch. I like a little meat on my woman. I have a cleaning lady to do that. And, for me the deal sealer, let *me* cook for *you* tonight.

I know what you're thinking, oh ye of little faith. Such a man does not exist. But I am keeping my eye on the horizon. I know he is out there. Hope springs eternal in this old sagging breast.

Eating at God's Table

In the 90's I had a kitchen so small my regular sized table wouldn't fit. So, I had a local craftsman custom-make a table for it. My new table was light oak wood with slate rock inlays. On each corner were pastel blue tulips with pastel pink leaves. Losing my house and everything to fire in the late 80's had made me hesitant to get attached to tangible things, but I loved that little table.

Then DeAnne had an extended hospital stay at The Medical University of South Carolina in Charleston, and I had to move down there. Because I couldn't afford to maintain living quarters in two separate towns, I eventually had to give up my apartment and put my things in storage.

After months in the hospital, she was finally released, but by then I had no home to return to. I searched frantically for a house I could afford. Some friends offered us their mother's house – she was in a nursing home - for an extremely low rent. It was completely furnished, and they didn't want to get rid of her things. So, I had to get rid of mine.

Another friend, who owned a consignment shop, offered to sell my furniture without taking a commission. He sold everything but the table, said no one was interested in it because it was so small. My heart was relieved. None of the other items meant much to me, but I hated the thought of losing my beautiful little table.

When I went to retrieve it, he met me smiling and handed me ninety dollars. "After I called you, a man came by and bought it," he said, happy to have made more money for me.

I went home and sat on my porch crying. That little table had been all I had left. But, as my mom had taught me, I sucked it up. God had been good to me. DeAnne was better. It was silly to mourn the loss of something as trivial as a table.

After a few years I moved out of the furnished rental house and was able to have my own furniture again. I had two hundred dollars budgeted for a table and went looking for the craftsman who had made the table I had lost so many years before.

He had stopped making furniture but sent me to his brother who was also a craftsman. Nothing in his shop interested me. Then I saw some tabletops leaning against a wall. I went to check them out and there it was - a larger version of my tiny slate rock table with the same pastel flowers and wooden oak frame.

Excited, I asked him, "Can you put legs on this for me?"

"Sure," he said. "I'll even make seat covers in any color you want for the chairs."

My mind went to my almost empty bank account. A hand-crafted table and four chairs with custom covers. I knew I wasn't going to be able to swing that. Still, I took a deep breath and asked, "How much?"

He rubbed his chin, looked at the pieces, then said, "How about two hundred?"

It's almost twenty years old now. Although I've sold, given away and bought lots of furniture since then, the table stays. I'll never get rid of it. It's a reminder of how much God loves me. When Doug wanted to replace it last year, I told him the story of how I got it.

"You may not have known it," I told him, "But you've been eating at God's table all these years."

Getting Ready to Lift and Stretch

I was chatting with a few friends a couple of months ago, and the discussion turned to what we could do to improve our health. The conversation touched on eating more salads, drinking water, limiting salt, and exercise. Feeling very self-righteous I informed them I was a member of the gym.

I could see the astonishment on the faces of most of the group, and along with the surprise, a touch of admiration. Then a girl who knew me well piped up from her end of the couch, "Jean, it's not enough to be a member. You have to go."

I am not lazy by any means. Nor am I a couch potato. I rarely turn on my television. I push-mow my lawn in the summer. And I go dancing every weekend. I just have a love/hate relationship with exercise equipment.

I have analyzed the problem and reached the conclusion that my goal-oriented personality has trouble exercising for the sake of exercise. I need a concrete target. Riding a bicycle that reaches no destination seems futile. How can I feel good about riding ten miles if I climb off in the same spot I climbed on?

I am continuously trying to find fun ways to stay fit. My daughter bought me an exercise ball. I could not get the hang of that thing. I would position myself on my stomach only to topple over on my head. If I sat on it, it would roll out from under me.

In the beginning, I kept it in my bedroom, but the floor was unlevel. The ball never stayed where I put it. I would lie in bed waiting. I just knew it was going to roll up and stand patiently waiting for me to use it. Thoughts like that kept me from sleeping, so I put the ball in the kitchen broom closet.

The folding doors wouldn't close properly because it was too big for the closet. Although unable to see the ball anymore, I could still feel it lurking behind the door. I finally stored it in the garage.

I bought one of those things you stand on with a heavy spring ending in a handle. Some movie star advertised it on television as the perfect piece of exercise equipment. The only thing I gained from using it was the knowledge that big blue foot holders will leave bruises when they slap you upside your head.

In the past ten years, I have joined four gyms. The first one was small and didn't have much equipment. The second one was better, and even provided members with a personal trainer. My personal trainer was a size six redhead.

One day while she had me on a piece of equipment which made my torso twist in abnormal positions, I asked how long it took to acquire those firm arms, flat tummy, and curvy legs. She laughed heartily and replied, "Oh I was born with good genes. I've never had any trouble maintaining my figure."

I stiffened my body to keep from slapping the cutie and pulled a muscle in my back. I never returned to that particular gym after recovering from my injury. It wasn't the pain that made me give up. It was that perky redhead.

The third gym I joined had everything a person needed to stay fit. I signed up, received my key, bought some cute gym pants, and felt really good about the whole situation. One day about a month after joining, I decided to visit my new gym for a look-see.

The girl at the front desk offered me a towel. I smiled at her naivety - I had no intention of working up a sweat. I peeked into the main part of the gym and sauntered down to the aerobics class. The room was glass enclosed, so I never made it inside.

Those women were working so hard, it made me tired just watching. I smiled at the girl behind the desk as I left. After that I would drive through the parking lot once in a while to make sure they were putting my money to good use.

Last Spring, I joined Fitness World in Cheraw. It was perfect for me. There are so many machines I never have to wait to use one. I can go anytime I want. And - one of its best features - the Raw Town Coffee Shop is within walking distance. Have you tasted their shakes?

I did quite well for a few months. Then life got in the way, and once again my gym became my main charity. I donated money every month and felt guilty every time I drove by. Billy from Fitness World came in this week. He told me he was running a special if I wanted to join.

The owner of my gym has no idea I'm a member. It's time to change things. Besides, I have grown weary of the guilt I feel every time I pass Fitness World. My mind is made up. I'm going to stop driving through that part of town.

Good Sermon

When I worked in the office of a local grocery store, our ads in the local newspaper sometimes had misprints. One week, suitcases, twenty-four packs, of brand name beer were advertised at $1.49 instead of $14.99.

We weren't held to printer errors due to a disclaimer at the bottom of the ad, but we made sure there were large signs on the beer case with the correct sale price, put a sign at the entrance to the store, and even had one of the stockers red sticker the individual suitcases.

We had no problems until the end of the week. A cashier paged me because she was having difficulty dealing with a petite, elderly Sunday school teacher. The top and bottom of her shopping cart was jam-packed with suitcases of beer. In fact, that was the only thing in her cart.

When I arrived at the register, she was demanding the cashier let her have them at $1.49. For effect, she was stamping one tiny black-patent-leather clad foot. The poor cashier was so intimidated by this little lady, she felt she needed back-up.

For ten minutes I explained we had the right to correct printer errors, that the signs on the shelf had the correct sale price. For ten minutes she refused to accept my decision, shaking her head so hard, her flower decked hat was askew.

Suddenly, in the middle of her protesting, she shoved the cart into my midriff, told me to keep my beer, straightened her hat and turned away. Then she started talking animatedly to the lady who had pulled in line next to her. They started a heated discussion on the visiting preacher they were having the next day

I smiled at this act of divine intervention and pushed the beer to the back, stopping on my way to assure a gentleman in aisle nine that, even though the package said Tide Free, he still would be expected to pay for it.

Sometimes You Get a Dog

I joined an internet dating site when I was single, the free version, not the expensive in-depth one. It was just for fun. I had enough trouble dating in the real world. I for sure wasn't going to go out with someone I met online.

When I started dating a "real" man on a regular basis, I found out he was a paying member on the same site. I had closed my account, and he asked for my help in closing his. He had stopped paying for it, but neither of us could get it to close. Our only option was to deactivate it, which we did.

Unfortunately, he had trouble being a one-woman man or even a two-woman man. After about a year I ended the relationship. Single once more, I decided to check out Perfect Match again. Their policies had changed and, even for a free membership, I would have to give the site more information than I wanted to.

Then I had an a-ha moment that, in retrospect, I should have let pass. I decided to reactivate and use my ex's account. I had all his info, so it wasn't difficult at all. I just signed into his account, changed the gender from male to female - he had a name that could be a man or woman - and was good to go.

I uploaded my photo - he had never posted one. And as easily as that, I was ready to view my matches. I checked out about ten of the men, found no one interesting and went to change everything back and deactivate the account once again.

To my surprise, I couldn't delete the matches I had viewed. He had viewed around twenty women a couple of years before. They were still there. I had viewed half that many men, and the site had just added their profile pictures to the women's. They were all there - both men and women - smiling at me from the matches page, winking and sending emails.

What was supposed to be a sneak in, look around, and sneak back out venture had become a little complicated. I gave up on the coed matches and went back to the profile page to delete my photo. Perfect Match wouldn't let me. I could replace the photo, but not delete it.

I searched my pictures folder and found a photo of an ugly, old, yellow dog. Perfect. I uploaded him into the photo box. Satisfied with my choice, I left Perfect Match with that old dog lying in the sun staring disinterestedly at the camera, while both men and women winked at him.

Even though no one will ever thank me for it, at least I let the date hunters on Perfect Match know that when it comes to internet dating, sometimes you get a dog.

Discovering My Inner Booty

I met my children and their families near their homes in North Carolina for a much-needed family visit this week. When the eleven of us arrived at the restaurant, it was pure joy to see my grandkids come running to me.

Parker is almost as tall as I am, which isn't really a major accomplishment for an eleven-year-old. I'm just a tad over five feet. Lexie, my granddaughter, is nine, and amidst the hugs and kisses, I pointed out she resembled a cowgirl. Her grey skirt was western style, perfect for swirling, and she had on black boots.

As we walked together into the steak house, I said, "Baby, you look like you should be dancing the *Cotton Eye Joe.*"

We had been shown our table by this time, and there was an alcove nearby. Lex whirled into it and started doing the dance steps. I watched in astonishment. My little city born cowgirl was doing a line dance. She had learned it in gym.

Delighted that a school had come up with such an innovative way of teaching children to exercise, I joined her for a few steps. We sat down to give our order, but I asked if she knew the Cupid Shuffle, and we were off again.

There were many things that were taboo in our home when I was a young girl tiptoeing my way through an unrelentingly stern world. Of course, the major transgressions such as cards, gambling, pool, and liquor were clearly defined, but my father had a sub-category of minor sins we had to avoid, also.

One of the biggies was dancing. I skipped, hopped, jumped, twirled, did cartwheels, and hung by my knees from tree branches, but I was not allowed to dance. The closest I got was when I went next door to play with my friend Shirley, and her younger sister, Debbie. The three of us would lip sync to some of our favorite girl groups.

Because we were younger, and Shirley was bossy, Debbie and I never got to be anything but the back-up singers. A bit of swaying was involved in our backyard performance, but that wasn't considered a serious infraction.

Later, as a teenager, I surreptitiously did the fish, the jerk, the skate, and the swim at a friend's house one night. I agonized over my fall from grace as I tried to sleep that night, hoping my father wouldn't find out.

Upon reaching adulthood we must sift through the things we were taught as children, discard what doesn't work for us, and keep what does. Because there were so many rules in my childhood, I have spent a lifetime sifting.

I decided early on dancing around my kitchen made me happy, and life without music would be dull indeed. I twirled all my babies around, too, laughing as I swung them through the air.

Life takes some of us to a few out of the way places before bringing us home and, oddly enough, the little girl who wasn't allowed to dance has ended up traveling with a band. Over the years I have learned to hold my own on the dance floor with the baby boomer crowd.

However, I had never line danced, and the places we go have a lot of line dancing. Last month I heard a young woman was going to teach line dance/exercise classes at the town recreation center. I was jubilant. I called to sign up.

Now two nights a week I gather with a group of like-minded women of varying ages. And we dance. In the beginning had you asked if we thought we could, our answer would have been a resounding no.

Then it became a hesitant yes, and now we're beginning to pull it off. We slide, skate, shuffle, kick, twirl, rock, and walk it by ourselves. We talk, dance, and sweat, but most of all we laugh.

Because I am used to just dancing to the beat without worrying about steps, I am the worst student in the group, but our teacher is very patient with all of us. I think she's waiting for her ducklings to become swans.

I can slide, skate, shuffle, kick, twirl, rock and walk it by myself, just not in line with everyone else. I turn too much and end up facing the wall. I count four beats instead of three, and my booty...oh dear, my booty.

My journey in line dancing is only just beginning. I have never in my life danced in sync with a group. Well, to be honest with you, I don't really dance in sync with the group now. The teacher has to say, "Miss Jean, what are you doing now?" several times a night.

But she's working on us. Having finally gotten a roomful of women in touch with their inner booty, one would think the hard part was over. Not so, says our teacher. Now that my fellow dancers and I have rediscovered our booty, apparently, we must learn to scoot it.

Message From God

One Sunday when I was eating with my family at Bill's BBQ in Cheraw, I ran into a guy I hadn't seen in thirty years. My niece had dated him right out of high school. He asked if she was still married. When I told him no, he wanted her number.

I never give out people's numbers, so told him I would give his number to her. But he had left his cell in the car and couldn't remember his number. So, I gave him my number and told him to text his to me.

A few hours later, he called me all excited. I waited politely for him to calm down. Finally, he said, "Jean, God just told me he sent you to me, that you're the one I'm supposed to be with."

I held my phone away from my ear, looked to make sure it was the same guy. You need to be certain in matters like that. Then I busted his spiritual bubble. "I'm sorry, "I told him. "I'm on pretty good terms with God, and I am positive He would have let me know if he was going to be sending me to someone."

The Right Call

When I was a scan manager my boss would always send me out of the office to handle any problems that cropped up. He said he could always trust me to make the right call. One day a woman drove smack dab into one of our tall parking lot lights with a huge cement base.

My boss and I walked out together, but when the husband started yelling at him, the boss said, "You got this, right Jean?" Then he skedaddled back inside.

The man was very emphatic that it was my company's fault for putting the light there. I looked at the car which was still up against the base of the light. I looked at the screaming man, who reeked of alcohol in the middle of the day. I looked at the woman, then stepped a bit closer to her. Yep, she reeked, too.

I told the man to calm down. He yelled, "I'm not gonna calm down until you call somebody with more authority than you got. We gonna need some money to fix this car. And I want this pole moved. It shouldn't have been there in the first place. If y'all hadn't put it there, my wife wouldn't a hit it."

Since I had already assessed the situation, I told the man he was right. I was going to call someone with more authority than I had. I pulled my cell phone out of my pocket, called a policeman friend, told him I had a problem, could he come to my workplace. He said sure. The screaming man who had no idea I had called a cop, started smiling, told me that was more like it.

He leaned back against the car with his arms crossed, asked who I had called and how long would it be before they got there. I matched his smile and raised him one, "I called the police. They're just down the street, so they'll be here any moment, and they certainly have more authority than either one of us."

The man's mouth snapped shut, he looked around, saw someone he knew, waved them down, got in their car and left. I looked at his wife. She looked at me, climbed back in her car, backed it away from the pole and left, too.

I guess I made the right call.

Cantaloupes and Candy

I believe dating is like buying a cantaloupe. I can smell them, thump them, and check their color. I still never know what they'll be like once I open them up. Price doesn't matter. Place of origin doesn't matter. Looks don't matter. I never know what I'm going to get. And I seldom get a good cantaloupe.

Truth is I never managed to get the hang of dating. It seemed to involve a lot of pretense. And I'm not good at pretending. Life has turned me into a realist with no time to waste on trying to figure out who someone really is. Just like with the cantaloupes, I was terrible at picking out which men to date. As a result, I didn't date a lot, wasn't good at it, didn't like it.

At some point, the fact that I had shed my sweet Southern womaness when my first marriage collapsed usually led to complications in new relationships. During my third or fourth, or maybe it was fifth or sixth attempt at trying to forge a relationship with someone, I made my biggest blunder ever. Although I have trouble saying that with a straight face.

I had just moved to the town my new man friend lived in. This was during the days we only had landlines, so I had to change phone companies. The young lady at the front desk did not understand my request, kept telling me the phone was already connected. It was, but in the last resident's name. The lineman came in while we were going back and forth, grasped the situation immediately and took care of it.

My unnecessarily long visit to the phone company made me late for my second, or third or fourth date with my newest fellow. I was still aggravated when I reached his place. This man I hardly knew sat quietly watching me while I paced back and forth in his living room complaining.

I stopped pacing long enough to look at him and say, "And to top it off, guess what her name was? Without giving him a chance to answer, I said, "It was Candy. She's certainly not going to grow up to be President, is she? No sir, not with a name like that."

I finished my tirade with, "What kind of mother would name her daughter Candy?"

I didn't really expect a response, but my soon-to-be-former boyfriend cleared his throat and said quietly, "My ex-wife."

I Think It's About Forgiveness

Tony was nineteen when we married. I was sixteen. My Dad had died two months earlier, and Tony held me in his lap, arms wrapped tightly around me while I cried. Without either of us realizing, he took my father's place that day.

When we married, our first home was so small, we couldn't run the fan on the heater in the wintertime because it was too hot. There were many more homes after that in many different towns. Tony was looking for his mission, his calling, his niche in life. He never found it.

But he was always searching for it.

He thought it would be in the next town, around the next bend in the road. Like a dutiful wife, I followed his dreams with him. After all, it was the journey that mattered, not the destination.

After the birth of our first child, Tony found a job working nights. It paid well, but he hated it. He missed the baby and me and spent his breaks composing totally inane poetry for us on brown paper towels. He said it wasn't poetry unless it rhymed, so he would use any words that rhymed whether they made sense or not.

While he worked, I stayed home and played house. With real baby dolls. We presented a Ward and June Cleaver front to the world for over twenty years, but the crude seams that held the fabric of our lives together were slowly unraveling.

It would only be natural to question what went wrong, but the truth is it was never right. We began our lives while still children, incapable of choosing a life partner, trying to pretend we had made the right decision. We became adults during the marriage, and had a difficult time admitting we didn't belong together.

It took us twenty-two years, but we finally drew the curtain on our marriage. During the divorce we ran the gamut of breaking-up emotions, rejection, hurt, jealousy, resentment, and wounded pride. Tony and I never let those feelings turn into the hatred which consumes so many divorcing couples.

At first, we did try to place blame. It was his fault. It was my fault. And finally, truthfully, it was no one's fault. We forgave one another for real or imagined wrongs and went on to love again. Much of life revolves around loss. Often time it is the foibles of human beings, ignorant of the consequences of the decisions they make, which causes those losses.

The prefix ex when added to husband or wife carries distasteful connotations. I do not want Tony to be remembered that way. A true

Southern gentleman, he was charismatic and funny. Everyone liked him.

He enjoyed playing practical jokes and didn't mind being the butt of them. Always respectful, he opened doors, carried packages, and never let other men say or do anything inappropriate around women and children. He was also the best friend anyone could have.

He loved to sing but, like the poetry, wasn't so good at it. However, his exuberance in the singing of the songs outweighed his vocal shortcomings. On the other hand, he really excelled in the games he enjoyed playing - chess, pool, monopoly, backgammon, dominos, and canasta.

He started projects, but never finished them. He planned grand things which never quite came to fruition. Unfazed, he kept planning. He always tried to do the right thing, failing often, but always trying.

He loved auctions, pigeons, his kids, his Mom, God, Mickey Smith, Harvey Griffin, Shellie Allen, coffee, a Doberman named Dixie, genealogy, Chesterfield County's history, The Civil War, big boobs (just being truthful), and Dolly Parton, (makes sense when you think about it).

I even think sometimes he loved me.

It was a crisply cold October day in 2003 when our oldest son called crying. Daddy had cancer, he said. Please come he said. I went. I sat in the hospital room with Tony and our four children. With unshed tears in our voices, we spent a couple of hours talking about our lives as a family. We laughed a lot, saving our tears for when we were alone.

I visited him for the last time in February 2004, three days before he left us. In a weak but strangely excited voice he told me he had seen where he was going. "It's not like we were taught," he whispered, "But it's beautiful".

Holding tightly to my arm, he talked feverishly, hurriedly, trying to fit everything in before the tiredness overtook him. As he talked, his words restored a faith I thought I had lost.

Dying is an event which transcends petty grievances and self-indulgent human emotions. I was thankful Tony and I had found the peace which comes with forgiveness long before this moment transpired.

We had loved and nurtured four children together. The bond still held. I smoothed his hair, kissed him gently on the forehead, told him I loved him, and made it to my car before the sadness engulfed me.

Martin Luther King said, "Man must evolve for all human conflict a method which rejects revenge, aggression, and retaliation. The foundation for such a method is love."

I wish we could all learn the lesson he tried to teach. Maybe that would slow down the losses, and we could celebrate more gains.

In memory of Tony Ford Smith 1949 – 2004

I Had a Dream

I grew up believing in dreams. My mom dreamed things that happened. She didn't do it often. She wasn't a medium, nor did she have ESP. She just occasionally, randomly dreamed things that came to pass.

On one of our visits from Georgia, Tony and I decided to take Little Tony and Kevin swimming on the way home. It wasn't until we had loaded the boys in the car, that she found out we were stopping by the local swimming hole.

She begged us not to take them. She had dreamed someone in the family drowned. "It was a girl in my dream," she told us. "But please be careful anyway."

I believed in my mom's dreams but didn't want to disappoint the boys. We took them swimming, but I was extremely attentive while they played in the water. The day after we arrived home, I received a phone call telling me a teenage cousin, my mom's niece, had drowned in a pond near her house.

Unlike my mom's dreams, mine had no substance to them. Even though they were extremely detailed, they were usually silly and meaningless. Like the night I dreamed I was Wonder Woman looking at comic books in the local drug store.

In my dream, two men with guns came in. I squatted down behind the magazine racks trying to hide, but realized I was a super heroine. I twirled three times and stood there wearing that beautiful suit.

Unfortunately, I was still short and skinny, and the suit was Lynda Carter's size. I had to hold it up, so couldn't get my hands free to save the store. To add insult to injury, even though I did my twirling just right, I found I had no super powers.

Holding the suit under my chin, I squatted back down as quietly as possible, so as not to disturb the robbers. I'm sure a dream interpreter would say I felt inadequate in real life, but I think it was just a case of too much television.

My mom's premonition dreams may be a family thing. My cousin Debbie called me when my boys were small just to ask if I were okay. Debbie and I weren't close, so it was an unexpected call. She said, in a voice filled with embarrassment, that she'd had a dream. "Oh no," I thought, "Another one."

She told me she had seen me dressed all in blue running down the sidewalk covered in blood. Since I was staying with my mom at the time, and she lived in town, Debbie's running down the street covered in blood dream was scary stuff for a believer like me.

Not long after the conversation with Debbie, four-year-old Tony fell face down on the bricks in Miss Hallie's flowerbed. He started bleeding profusely from his nose. I had no car, so grabbed him up and went running down the street to get help. By the time I got to the doctor's office my blue t-shirt and blue jeans were covered in blood.

My mom had dreams, my cousin had dreams, even my daughter had dreams that came true. I never did. Until I had a dream about my ex-husband Tony, father of my four children.

In my dream he was completely bald, dressed in army fatigues with a gun in each hand sitting in a cabin. Some strangely shaped creatures, not animal or human, were trying to get in through the boarded-up door and windows. His cabin was a façade. Just like the buildings on a movie set, it had no back.

I was about to climb the hill to warn him when a man in white stopped. "You can't save him," he told me. "You have to take care of your children."

"But they'll get him," I cried.

"I know," he said, "I'll go to him." Then he repeated, "But you must stay down here and take care of the children."

A couple of months later, my oldest son called to tell me his dad had just found out he had cancer. The children and I went immediately to him. Four months later, I saw him for the last time. He clung to my arm, and we talked of many things, important things.

He assured me he was ready to go. "They came for me before," he said weakly, stopping to take short breaths, "And I wasn't ready. I was worried about the children. But they've shown me that you will take care of them, so I'm ready now."

It was long after he died that I remembered the dream. As with most dreams, it was useless. I couldn't save him in the dream world, and I couldn't save him in the real world. But I do know there was a man in white looking out for him, reassuring him, standing waiting for him.

I know.

I had a dream.

Blinded by the Dark

When I was diagnosed with diabetes, I researched the horror stories associated with the disease. I read about heart problems, amputations, nerve damage, skin infections, and loss of eyesight. Not long after the diagnosis, I woke in the middle of the night to pitch blackness.

I looked over at my clock – nothing. No light was shining through my bedroom window from the street light outside. Devastated to the point of nausea, I realized I had lost my sight. Talking myself out of a panic attack – I lived alone - I felt my way through the dining room into the kitchen and opened the refrigerator. I couldn't see anything in it.

Sick at heart I felt my way back into the bedroom to find my cell phone. I worried the whole way about how I was going to key the numbers in without my sight. I would have to do it by touch, I told myself. Reaching my nightstand, I felt around on it, found my phone, and flipped it open.

The screen lit up.

I found out the next day a big storm had caused a power outage all over town. I was so tired I had slept through it.

Just Breathe

Many years ago, I managed a store that contained, among other things, a small but very nice restaurant. One day a server called in sick and another didn't show up. I was left with a sweet, but inexperienced young girl who panicked on me.

I took her by both shoulders, looked in her eyes, and told her, "You can do this. Just stand still for a moment and breathe...breathe in and breathe out."

I was trying to distract her from focusing on a room full of hungry people by encouraging her to take it one table at the time. My ploy worked. She calmed down.

Unfortunately, the owner heard me telling the panicked waitress to breathe. She asked for a word with me in private. We stepped outside of the restaurant. She was angry. Her words were clipped and sharp.

At the end of her tirade, she yelled, "How dare you tell her to breathe! I hired her to wait on my customers, not to breathe." Just as I had distracted the harried waitress, I distracted the owner from her anger. I did it by quitting. I just couldn't work a job where employees weren't allowed to breathe

Don't You Like the Cat?

Beautiful weather is here, and it's time to haul the grill out of storage. I love the flavor of grilled foods. Rib eyes, hot dogs, corn, skewered vegetables - my mouth is watering as I type. Unfortunately, I have never mastered the manly art of grilling out.

The human male seems to be born with the knowledge of how to place the charcoal for maximum burn effect, how much lighter fluid to squeeze per briquette, and exactly the precise moment to remove the food so that is perfectly cooked.

I am convinced it is a gender thing. That is the only reason I can think of to explain why I cannot grasp the technique. Until twenty years ago. I had never needed to have a working knowledge of the grill. I had a husband who handled the man stuff.

Then I joined the ranks of the divorced and had to do many things formerly considered a man's job. I acquired enough knowledge to get me by in some areas and excelled in a few. From the beginning, I realized grilling was not going to be one of my success stories.

I first glimpsed my ineptness when the guys left me in charge of the grill while they made a run to the local store. They were very reluctant to do so, but I convinced them I could handle it. At no time did they mention taking the sizzling burgers up. My only instructions were to keep turning them.

I turned those delectable little pieces of red meat until they looked exactly like the briquettes, black and charred. We ordered take out, and I was never left in charge of the grill again.

Because of my love for things grilled, it was almost a necessity to keep a man in my life. This wasn't always possible, though. Some say it is because I am fiercely independent. However, I think I have been mislabeled.

In my years of being single I have learned men don't do well in captivity, so I try to leave them free to roam the open range, just roping one in occasionally to fire up the grill for me.

During one of the manless periods in my life, with more foreboding than hopefulness, I decided to grill out. I did something dreadfully wrong this time. It could have been brushing the sauce on the raw meat before I laid it on the grill or using too much lighter fluid.

In mentally sifting through the evidence later, I am convinced it was not waiting for the charcoal to turn gray. In my defense, I couldn't see what color the charcoal was because of the nice big flame I had going.

At any rate, that big flame became even bigger when I put my pork chops on. My spray water bottle needed reinforcements. Nine-year-old DeAnne ran to bring the hose back from the garden, barely getting it there in time to put out the fire.

The pork chops were ruined. DeAnne and I passed on them, but twelve-year-old Aaron valiantly tried to make me feel better by eating one. The sound he made crunching on that burned meat made my Momma heart proud.

I usually learn from the mistakes I can bring myself to admit, but for some reason, last week I decided to give it one more try. Fifteen years had passed since the pork chop debacle, and I wanted something grilled. I have a small one-foot smoker grill on my back porch.

I called Doug, the buyer of the grill, for advice. He explained to me about stacking the charcoal, putting fluid on each briquette, waiting for it to saturate, then lighting it. He was so good at explaining the grilling process to me, that I was very confident this time. I could almost taste that pork chop.

As my son's cat wound itself in and out of my legs, mewing for attention, I stacked the charcoal. However, remembering the fire that destroyed my grill and eyebrows last time, I stood way back, squirting lighter fluid and throwing matches.

The cat was a distraction, and so was my neighbor who had come out to sneak a smoke but stayed to watch my matches spiral through the air. I could only imagine what my antics looked like to him, because my solid porch railings prevented him from seeing the grill.

After six or seven attempts, I couldn't get the fire to start, and the cat was getting excited. I picked up the lighter fluid, matches, and cat. My neighbor yelled across his fence, asking me what was wrong.

I yelled back as I reached to open the door, "I've tried and tried to get it to burn. I keep squirting the lighter fluid and throwing the matches, and I'm getting a little frustrated. I'm just going to use the oven.

He gave me a strange look, took another puff off his cigarette, and yelled back. "Don't you like the cat?"

Getting What I Paid For

Years of raising children on my income alone taught me to be very conservative with my money. Anything I could do myself instead of paying a professional helped me stay within my budget. The financial strain left home with the last child, but by that time conservatism was deeply imbedded in my lifestyle.

One of the ways I tried to save money was by avoiding the beauty shop whenever possible. I cut my own hair for years, and I was over fifty before the gray became a problem. When it did, true to my nature, I decided to dye it myself.

My daughter, DeAnne, was a young teenager at the time, but had already started changing her hair color to suit her mood. She helped guide me through the myriad mass of colors. I was just a little hesitant about entrusting my hair to her, because at the time her dark black eyebrows had scabs on them.

She was living life as a gothic and had colored her hair jet black like Morticia Addams. Being a perfectionist she also decided to do her eyebrows. The dye didn't follow the shape of the brow line, causing her to resemble a feminine Groucho Marx.

When the conventional soap and water didn't remove it, my little sweetie tried to scrub it off using a toothbrush laced with comet. The dye stayed, but the skin left. Amazingly, she chose the right color for me and did a great job applying it. I was hooked on do-it-yourself hair dye.

Until last week, with one or two, three or four – five at the most - exceptions, I have had good results doing my own color. After buying a closeout unknown brand dye for three dollars which melted my hair strands together, I learned to pay a little more and get the quality stuff.

The brand I have used all these years only let me down once, and that was just a fluke. There wasn't enough mixture, but I tried to dye anyway. This resulted in half dry, half wet partially dyed hair. I pulled on a sweat shirt and headed back to Wal-Mart, thinking I could sneak in and out quickly, because it was nearly closing time.

I managed to get in without anyone noticing me, but the associate at the service desk refused to exchange it for me. She insisted on giving me my money back, telling me I would have to buy it again. I leaned over the counter and said in a near whisper, "You don't understand. I don't have on underwear".

Even that did not sway her. She would not give into my pleas. Old Sam would have been proud. After receiving my refund, I retrieved a new box from the shelf, and almost reached the checkout unobserved when a reader spotted me. He yelled something about my most recent column causing the few late shoppers to take notice of me. Totally humiliated, I paid for my dye and slunk out.

Everything went smoothly until a couple of weeks ago when my man friend suggested I get highlights in my hair. "Do you know how much that would cost?" I told him.

Refusing his offer to pay – I am an independent cuss – I checked out the do-it-yourself-kits. There were only two that also contained the dye. One was blonde, and the other was cherry truffle. That sounded like a beautiful color to me.

I rushed home, read the directions, put the color on, waited the allotted time, washed the dye out, and dried my hair. Oh my goodness – the color was a deep rich mahogany with purple running through it. After the shock wore off, I had a brilliant idea. I would put highlighter all over it, thus lightening the color. My hair came out Clemson orange.

I called my son Aaron, and, unable to keep the panic out of my voice, informed him I needed help fast. He arrived almost immediately but stepped back in shock when I opened the door. He couldn't help what he said next but apologized right away. He didn't hesitate when I asked him to buy brown dye for me, even though he had to drive twenty miles at eleven at night.

I applied it the next morning, and had the most awesome colors. I looked like a spice girl. Well actually like all the spice girls rolled into one. My hair was deep auburn with purple highlights, a touch of yellow, and a hint of rich brown. Kind of funky punk. I had to wear it to work, but dyed it brown as soon as work was over. This time I looked like I had visited the Willy Wonka chocolate factory.

A few applications of Selsun Blue worked a miracle, and I am now a redhead. In two days I ran the gamut of hair color and spent fifty-four dollars and thirty-two cents on my hair. If it's true you get what you pay for, I should look better.

I Wrote a Poem

When I was fifteen a new boy came to Chesterfield High School. His name was Tim. He was a good looking young man with extremely white teeth and hair the color of a raven's wing when the sunlight hits it just right.

My friends would watch that gorgeous hair fall over his brow as he talked. When he brushed it back with a quick swipe of his hand, a collective, though inaudible sigh would go up from the girls gathered around him.

A few of us thought his nose was too long, but the rest agreed it went perfectly with his dark skin. He was more well-dressed than the boys we had grown up with, too. His pants were crisply pressed with a sharp crease down both legs, and he wore color-coordinated cardigans over dress shirts.

Tim joined our group by default. The different cliques in our school formed circles before homeroom. When he entered the building from the front, we were the first kids he encountered. We were a friendly bunch, so he stood talking with us in the mornings before the bell rang.

Even though we welcomed his presence, we realized it was only a matter of time before he learned we weren't the cool kids at Chesterfield

High. We weren't misfits, but we weren't fitter-inners either.

Eventually, as expected, it dawned on him that there wasn't a cool one amongst us. Naturally, he went searching for his own kind. He hadn't even stayed long enough for most of the group to mourn his passing.

Nevertheless, during his short sojourn with us one of my friends fell for him. She kept her adoration so hidden, no one noticed, especially not Tim. Still, she was heartbroken when he distanced himself from us.

To show I empathized with her – I, too, was a victim of unreturned adoration - I wrote a sad poem about unrequited love. Looking back, it probably made her feel even worse. On the other hand, fifteen-year-olds thrive on drama, so maybe she appreciated it.

After Tim moved away, and my friend's heart had mended, I submitted the poem to *Teen Magazine*. They printed it. I was proud. My mom was proud. The magazine was put away and forgotten. Several years after the first poem, *Teen* requested a poem with a bicentennial theme.

I wrote a topical poem about America's youth. When the magazine came out, my poem went sort of seventies viral. High school yearbook committees all over the United States requested permission to use it as their theme. To show their appreciation they sent me copies.

Last week my son asked about the second poem, *The Spirit of '76*.

All but one of the yearbooks had burned in a fire that destroyed our home in the eighties, and I couldn't locate my copy of the magazine. I turned to that glorious invention, the internet.

I didn't find *The Spirit of '76* but, out of curiosity, I put the title of the first poem Teen had printed in the search engine and sat on my bed at one in the morning amazed. *A Love to Call My Own* was alive in cyberspace.

It was used as an example of how to write a love poem, entered in poetry contests under other people's names and posted on personal websites as the property of the owners. It was on a website for those who had been in love with cheaters.

Several men even claimed authorship for this love poem written by a teenage girl. It was posted on a prison blog site from the girlfriend of an inmate to her incarcerated beloved. I guess the inmate had one too many conjugal visitors.

There were those who considered themselves poetry aficionados. They took it apart, analyzed every line, gave it glowing praise. One of these pretentious posters said it was utterly passionate, that it enlightened his heart to croon. I wanted so badly to tell him I was fifteen when I wrote it. I had no idea what passion was.

I contacted one site owner because it had been entered in their poetry contest, and the person who stole it was gushingly appreciative of the compliments MY poem received. That one irritated me. When faced with the fact it had been copyrighted by *Teen*, the owner took it down.

Finally, on one site a woman told them they were all lying. She said it existed before the date people claimed to have written it, that it was from a magazine in the early seventies. She had found the clipping in her sister's school book back then and memorized it word for word. She asked the real author to step forward.

I didn't respond. It was futile to claim authorship of a forty-year-old poem. It would have been impossible to track them all down, to correct them all. No one would know who I was, and I was leery of giving my personal information out.

I was fifteen. I wrote a poem. Before computers, before the internet, before websites. The magazine is gone, but the printed word is a powerful tool. It endures. Forty years later, *A Love to Call My Own* is still resonating with people. Since I am not credited as the author on any of the sites, I shall have to be anonymously proud.

Out of the Darkness

There was something about the darkness that terrified me as a child. It was a palpable, breathing thing to me. As soon as I stepped into the obscurity of the night, the world of light and the people who inhabited it vanished. I tried to avoid being alone in the dark whenever possible.

One autumn night, when I was eight, an older relative took his daughter and me Snipe hunting. He explained this kind of hunting could only be done at night, and our older brothers had refused to help, so we were enlisted.

We were made to stand under a tree in the woods holding a brown paper bag, waiting for a Snipe to fall into it. When we caught one we were supposed to close the bag quickly and yell for J.C. We were frightened, cold, and we had no idea what a Snipe was.

Those Snipes never came, and we were too young to recognize we were the butt of a practical joke played on unsuspecting children in the rural South. We were chosen because we were more gullible than the boys. We were just glad the Snipes stayed away, we didn't ask any questions. This incident only increased my fears.

Last week I remembered that anxious vigil as I stood leaning against the side of a closed grocery store in the predawn hours. A reader told me about an early morning gathering he had been observing.

They've been doing it for six weeks, he informed me excitedly. They won't hang around much longer. He wanted me to investigate and write about it in my column. I felt his urgency as he said, "Just watch for them - they will come. They always come."

According to him, the group assembled in the trees across the street under cover of darkness. So, like in my Snipe hunting days, here I stood waiting. Although it was dark, I was able to see shapes because of the gleam of lights from the parking lot in front of the store.

Across the street behind another building the still fully leaved trees were in shadow, hulking and intimidating, as if they too were waiting. Despite being ashamed of the feeling, I was too apprehensive to walk closer. Nevertheless, the thrill of anticipation fueling this lookout overshadowed the apprehension.

Determined to investigate my reader's story, I squelched the urge to return to my car. I don't write about things like this, I reasoned. I write about the humorous, the nostalgic, and the ups and downs of everyday life. My stories are funny, not frightening.

But his impassioned plea reverberated in my head. I knew they were there in the darkness lurking. "Find out why," he pleaded. "Tell everyone. You can do it." So here I stood, shivering in the crisply cold morning air waiting.... like the trees.

Doubt assailed me. Maybe I should have asked someone to accompany me on this early morning mission. Thirty tension-filled minutes later, as the sable sky turned to gray, I heard a noise, then another.

The sound was faint, difficult to identify. If it came from the trees, I couldn't tell. It would have escaped my notice had I not been listening for it. Minutes went by with no more sounds. With the coming of the dawn both my apprehension and anticipation were diminishing.

Arms wrapped around my body to ward off the cold, I walked to the front of the store, determined to give up my post. I had done my best. No one could fault me. Or could they.

I saw a lone bird pecking disinterestedly at something in the almost empty parking lot. A shiver of a different kind went through me.... shades of Alfred Hitchcock. What was the bird doing there? The parking lot was clean. There was nothing for a foraging creature to find.

Laughing at this flight of fancy, I turned and headed back to my lookout. A few people on their way to work glanced questionably at me, but I smiled and walked on, moving ever closer to the trees, acting with a boldness I did not feel.

There. I heard it again... the same noise as earlier.... and another... and another. I paused. Had they heard me? Now the air filled with a strange yet familiar cadence. I wanted to run, but waited staunchly for what I knew would come.

Suddenly they came flying from the trees, out of the darkness into the light and, though I was vastly outnumbered, I stood my ground. This was indeed a story worth telling. I gasped. No longer afraid, just delighted at such orchestrated movement.

There was no flapping of wings, and their voices were mute. Perhaps it was their scouts I heard earlier speaking in language humans cannot understand. Like black snowflakes, they drifted silently across the sky and disappeared from my view.

Just like that, the birds were gone, altogether in one body. My reader's questions - Where did they come from? Where were they going? Why did they come back to this place day after day? What drew them here? Was this all or were there others? - would go unanswered.

As I stood there in awe, I knew I would tell the story...... just maybe not the way he wanted me to.

Happy Halloween everyone!

'Tis the Season to be Grateful

A friend on Facebook started a what are you thankful for round, and as I read the posts, I realized people, with small variations, are thankful for the same things. Like all of them, I am grateful for my children, my mother, good friends, good health, and all the cliché but true blessings we usually take for granted. It is expected that we should say a thank you God for these gifts.

With this in mind, I decided to dig beneath the surface of traditional giving of thanks and attempt to convey what I am most thankful for this Thanksgiving season. I poured a glass of tea and sat in the rocking chair on my back porch pondering my life in general and thankfulness in particular.

There was a breeze blowing the random leaves that were still falling, and as it playfully tousled my hair, I realized how truly content I am with life. How I arrived at this level of happiness formed the basis for my what I am thankful for list.

First of all, I am thankful for not having much. Having much is accompanied by all sorts of encumbrances, physical and emotional, in addition to financial. Life has outdone itself in teaching me lessons on having too much. Especially how attaching too much importance to the appropriation of the tangible can distract a person from acquiring the intangible.

Inanimate objects have always and will continue to be important to people. I used to have so many things, I needed a storage building to hold the ones the attic could no longer contain. Losing my home twenty years ago opened my eyes to the truth about possessions. Twenty years of accumulation can be gone in a two-mile trip to the store.

Now I think it's okay for a little girl to make mud pies with a frilly Sunday dress on. A coffee table is the perfect place to set drinks, candy and messy cookies. Spilling coke on new carpet is trivial, and dirty water left from melting snow on a clean kitchen floor makes me smile.

Another major gift I am thankful for is having my children watch me struggle with the adversities of life, especially the financial ones. They saw me work two jobs to provide them with necessities. It taught them not to expect other people to pick up their slack. No matter how heavy the load, fulfilling your responsibilities brings rewards of a special kind.

I am thankful for the sense of humor which has allowed me to live my life with more joy than sadness. Sometimes the losses in my life have outweighed the gains, but I have managed to not get sidetracked by this inequality. It isn't what we go through in life that damages us. It is our attitude toward it.

This may seem strange, but I am thankful for having loved and not been loved in return. The pain was great, but the experience was worth it. It has helped me define love more concretely. Genuine love is rare. If I am ever blessed to receive real love in a relationship, I will appreciate and treasure it.

In this same category, I am thankful that being hurt by loving the wrong person did not leave me bitter and depressed. I am glad to still have a heart that is open, because I have watched friends and family close down after finding love wanting. If true love enters my life, I will be the richer for it. If not, I will be no less rich for lack of it.

I am thankful that I have been able to access the forgiveness mode we have all been programmed with. People who cannot forgive stay angry all the time. I have found forgiveness to be a one-sided experience. Thus, I have learned to forgive without any expectation the one I am forgiving will change his or her attitude or feel regret for having harmed me.

I am also glad other people have been able to forgive me. We are all guilty of having wronged someone, not necessarily out of spite - often times out of ignorance.

Finally, the biggest blessing of all is the ability to forgive me. So many times, truly good people waste years of their lives regretting things they've done. This casts a shadow that changes the way they interact with others in all kinds of relationships. Self-forgiveness is a major key to being happy.

And so, my thanksgiving wish for you is that you invest your heart in things that give good returns, keep your sense of humor when life lets you down, and give yourself a break when you feel you've fallen short. Don't take life so seriously. After all, it isn't permanent.

Santa Baby

Santa Baby, with only a few lapses here and there, I have been a good girl most of my life. Before you contest this statement, let me say, in my defense, I did not know the dead rat would burst and create such a mess.

And although the birthday cake decorations may have been a little unorthodox, ants are considered a delicacy in some cultures. Shouldn't the fact that they went undetected when the cake was cut and eaten count in my favor?

Yes, I understand leaving eighteen bogus messages on someone's answering machine might be considered harassment, but they were untraceable. Now, Santa, you know what I threatened to do to my boss was physically impossible. Therefore, it falls under the realm of fantasy, and who knows more about fantasy than you, Santa.

This Christmas I am in need of a few things, and for a man of your unparalleled talents – this is called butt-kissing in the south - my humble requests would probably be as easy as a snap of your fingers. With that said, I submit to you my Christmas list.

My first request is for a pair of jeans which will fit around the vicinity of where my waist once was. After shopping for new jeans, I have become frustrated with what the department stores have to offer. The ones I tried on wouldn't reach my belly button, no matter how hard I tugged. They're only long enough from crotch to waist to rest uncomfortably on what, twenty years ago, were my hips.

Santa, darling, if I wear these new-styled jeans, I would be unable to bend over, squat (I'm not saying I can still squat – this is just for argument's sake), or even sit without sharing more than is decent with those around me.

This next request, my dear Santa, is totally selfish. Well, all of my requests are selfish, but this one probably takes the cake, no pun intended. Could I wake up thin tomorrow, please? The diets just aren't working, and exercise has proven to be an insurmountable obstacle. Okay, I'm the insurmountable obstacle, but either way it isn't getting done. Bring me a miracle, please.

Next - and I know this will be a bit more difficult - if you can't handle the waking-up-thin request, could you alter the world's vision of me? Instead of a short, dumpy, fiftyish grandma, I would like for people to see a slim, long-legged forty-year-old hottie.

I know making me look like a twenty-three-year old would be too big a stretch for even you, so I won't even ask. On second thought, just make me look like a slim, long-legged forty-year-old. I can pull the hottie part off on my own.

On Christmas Day, Santa, I would like to receive a call from my children, thanking me for everything I have ever done for them – no, let's change that. Everything would require too much time and eat up the minutes on everyone's phones.

Maybe they could just give honorable mention to the thirty-two thousand, eight hundred and fifty-two meals I've prepared, the tens of thousands of loads of clothes I've washed, the mileage I put on twenty-two different cars, the mileage they put on me, and, oh, never mind, this one's too difficult even for you.

My final request concerns your visit on Christmas Eve, and could be part B of number three on my list. When you jump down the chimney, could you land at the bottom as a six-foot tall, well-built, lightly tanned, forty-year-old?

That red suit is passé, and your beard is way too bushy. I don't even want to discuss those eyebrows. I'm sure you can pull this one off, because you are, after all, the grandfather of fantasy (more good old Southern butt-kissing).

After looking over this list, my hopes aren't high, so just do what you can, and I will understand. You are, after all, one busy old elf.

Thank you in advance,

Jean

PS

And Santa, for all of my readers out there, to thank them for a fantastic year and let them know I cherish the time I spent with them, please give them a holiday filled with the laughter of family, the entertaining companionship of friends, good food and great conversation, and warm homes and hearts. Also, if it isn't too much trouble, please wrap all of this in love before delivering. Merry Christmas!

Time to Dust Off Those New Year's Resolutions

Thanksgiving is just a memory, Christmas festivities are over, and, now, like Captain Kirk's Enterprise, we are on an unchangeable course toward New Year's at warp speed. There is no time to dally. We must pull out those New Year's resolutions, dust them off, and try again this year.

Of course, in saying this, I am assuming most of you are like me. Yes, I confess. I just pull the same ones out every year, because with a few minor alterations, my resolutions have been virtually the same since 1994.

At the top of my list, and everyone else's, according to reliable internet sources, is the resolution to lose weight. Although I resolve to do this at other times during the year, such as right after Thanksgiving and Christmas, and before every party and high school reunion, on New Year's I actually put it in writing.

Granted, since I started recycling my resolutions, the ink on the paper is faded in spots, and there are water damages. At my age, memory cannot be trusted, but I am almost positive the water damages were caused by my tears.

You see, years ago, I thought it was about keeping the resolutions, and was bitterly disappointed when I was unable to cross even the first one off. When it finally dawned on me that you get a do-over every January 1st, my attitude changed. Failure was an option.

Even with that insight, I still tried to keep the weight loss one. There was a new diet every year. I did the high protein diet, the cabbage soup diet, the four on and three off diet, and, my personal favorite, the eat everything you want and still lose weight diet. In case you didn't know, those people just flat out lied to us.

Every time a new diet failed, well-meaning family and friends tried to commiserate. My mom was the most consistent, but she only had one line of encouragement for me – "You look so much better with some fat on you. Skinny women just look sick."

I cheered up the first time my elderly boss said I looked better than I ever had. However, he finished that sentence with, *since you gained all that weight.*

The year of my divorce party, I was determined to get into a smaller size. After all, I was back on the market, and there was a lot of competition in the dating arena. The diet didn't work, but I had already purchased the skin-tight jeans. Skin tight is really a misnomer. Those jeans were tighter than my skin.

On the night of the party, I lay down on my back to zip them and practiced shallow breathing because the air wouldn't go down as far as usual. I couldn't sit down, dance, or make long sentences, but I smiled proudly all night long, just knowing I got into my new jeans.

Children can crush your ego and skip blithely on when it comes to weight. I used to teach a preschool Sunday school class. One morning, I added a new teaching tool, the flannel board. As the children watched, I placed pictures representing prominent people in the community on the new board.

There was a mommy and daddy, a policeman, a teacher, a fireman, and a minister. I explained who each picture represented and described what they did in terms the children could understand. I saved the picture of a group of children until last. As I placed it on the board, my question to the children was, "Who do you think is more important to God?"

I had noticed from the beginning of the lesson that one of my four-year-olds was watching me intently. I was encouraged by this and did a magnificent job that morning. When I posed my question at the end of the lesson, she waved her hand excitedly. My new star pupil, on her way to becoming teacher's pet, was making me so proud.

"Yes, Amanda," I said, smiling largely.

"Miss Jean," she said, as if it were a revelation, "If you didn't wear that belt, you wouldn't look so fat."

Deflated, I wrapped up the lesson, handed the children over to their parents, and took the belt off before entering the sanctuary.

I am prepared for this New Years. I have retyped my resolutions, so they're more legible. I added a couple of easy-to-keep ones just to make me feel better. I went through my closet and got rid of the four different sizes of clothes I had in there.

Then I went shopping and bought new clothes in the wrong size to give me a target to shoot for. I am ready for the New Year. However, being a realist, I bought the clothes a size too large.

Randomness?

I was at my desk working on a column in 2009 and stopped to look out over my front yard. In that moment I knew, without any doubt, that Cheraw was not where I would spend the rest of my life. Unusual - because I was extremely happy in Cheraw.

Sometimes, like a trailer for a movie, we get a nudge, a hint, a feeling, our life is about to take a different path. I took that hint and ran with it. I decided since I would be leaving Cheraw the mountains would be a good place to live. I loved the mountains.

While I was checking out jobs and rental houses in some mountain towns, I went dancing. I heard a really good band. The band had a great steel and sax player. A seemingly random event, that dance, a small occurrence in my busy life.

Maybe when we get that nudge, that feeling, that hint of things to come, we should just wait and see what unfolds. What a wonderful life I would have missed out on had I taken a job in the mountains and missed that dance, that band, that steel and sax player......my husband.

Soft Southern Winds

Don Williams is gone, taking a piece of my past with him. "Good Ole Boys Like Me" is my favorite song by him. The line about the Live Oak trees gets me every time.

I married my high school sweetheart, Tony Smith. By the time we'd been married a decade, I had moved nineteen times, never staying anywhere long enough to grow anything. And I loved green stuff - trees, plants - anything green.

Finally, after my husband's stint in the army, we put a trailer on an acre of land my daddy had given me before he died. It had been loaned to a farmer, so I found myself living in the middle of a corn field.

But my young husband knew I longed for green stuff. One day he came in waving a deed, all excited. "I bought you green stuff," he yelled. "I bought you trees." And indeed, he had - ten acres of green stuff, beautiful green stuff.

We built a beach house on our land, so I could live up among the branches of my beautiful trees, many of them Live Oaks. And I got to stay there long enough to raise my two oldest children and give birth to two more children.

It was our last home together.

For there came a time when Tony went in one direction, the kids and I in another. The children grew up, Tony passed away too young, I grew older.

But when I listen to Don Williams sing "I can still hear the soft Southern winds in the Live Oak trees", my mind goes back to those days, and I can see my beautiful trees swaying gently in the wind. And if I go just a little further back I can see a young man named Tony waving a deed at me, smiling...

The First Time

I was riding back to Georgia with Tony, my young soldier husband, and two babies the first time I heard the country music star Billy Crash Craddock. The kids and I had been visiting my mom in South Carolina, and Tony had come to pick us up and take us home. The kids were sleeping in the back seat, Tony was somewhere off in his own thoughts, and I was lost in mine, not an uncommon thing during our marriage

Rub it In, started playing on the radio. It was probably Crash's most famous recording, but I had never heard of it or him. Breaking the silence, Tony said, "He sings that kind of dirty live." I was staring out the window at the time but turned to look at him in the darkened car. I was puzzled by his words. When had he seen Billy Crash Craddock live? We had never been to a concert. We were too poor.

I pressured him until he finally confessed that while I had been at my mom's he had taken his "girlfriend" to the Crash concert. I don't know if I was more upset that he had a girlfriend or that he had gone to a concert. I forgave him, something I would be expected to do often in the coming years, and we went on with our dysfunctional marriage. After two more kids and sixteen more years of forgiving, my husband left me for his latest girlfriend.

This month I will be celebrating the anniversary of my marriage to one of the original Dream Lovers, the man who was Billy Crash Craddock's steel and sax player. Yes, my present husband was onstage playing, that long-ago night in Georgia, while my first husband and his "girlfriend" sat and listened.

Irony? I think so. Karma? Perhaps. Either way today I love and am loved. And I can now smile at that young sad girl/woman riding through the night listening to Billy Crash Craddock sing *Rub it In* on the radio. If only she knew what I know, she would smile, too.

Green Stuff

I wrote a column in remembrance of Tony Smith, my husband for twenty-two years and father of my four children, near the anniversary of his death. It revolved around a conversation I had with him three days before his death.

A columnist is constrained by word count so the published story, of course, only contained a brief synopsis of our talk. Standing in the kitchen of my home in Greensboro, my thoughts went back to that last conversation in its entirety. I put a slice of bread in the toaster and let my thoughts carry me back to that day.

Hospice had told the family in November 2003 that it would only be a few days at the most. Possibly even twenty-four hours. Months passed and still he lingered. In the beginning I had seen him regularly, but his wife had asked me to stop coming. I respected her wishes and left them alone. This was their time. I understood that.

Then in February he asked to see me. We had been divorced almost fifteen years by then. Leaving the financial support of the kids to me, while he went on with his life, had caused a great hardship not just for me, but for our children as well. It was weighing heavily on him.

He had accepted the fact he was dying, and he needed to apologize.

I told him it was all water under the bridge, not to worry about it. I was standing beside the hospital bed his family had set up in the living room. We could see the yard from the big double window. "That's where I saw them first," he said, looking past me. "They were in the field across the road."

His voice was low, and his breathing was shallow, forcing him to talk slowly.

"Then they were in the yard. They moved, but not by walking."

"One day I looked out of the window, and they were on the porch."

"Then I opened my eyes, and they were beside my bed. They asked me if I was ready. Jean, I lied and told them I was, but they knew it was a lie. They told me I wasn't ready yet, and they left."

Three people, beings, whatever you choose to call them had come for him in November but left without him.

Coming back to the present, I spread peanut butter on my toast and looked out of my own double window at mine and Doug's lush green yard. I marveled that long before I came into his life, Doug had planted something so suited to me.

Flowers are beautiful, but I have always loved green growing things. That's what our yard is full of. Green stuff. I was going to mow, but a light rain was falling, and I would have to put it off.

Disappointed, I mentally rearranged my day. I was so appreciative of the fact that having to cancel the mowing because of rain was not as big a thing as it would have been years ago. When I was working two jobs just to pay the bills.

The rain blurred as I drifted back to the past. Tony squeezed my arm, not hard, he was extremely weak. "They're back, and I'm ready this time."

I had my mouth open to take a bite of my toast when the chill bumps started on my legs and moved up my body.

Because I remembered what he said next.

"I was worried about you and the kids," he said, still holding to my arm. "But they assured me you would take care of the kids, and Jean..."

He had to stop for breath. Just talking was wearing him out.

"Jean, they told me your life will be better than it has ever been."

I have a wonderful life here in Greensboro, NC. Happier than I have ever been, my gaze travels over this beautiful yard that looks like it was planted just for me. I listen to the man who loves me more than I've ever been loved piddling around in his music room, and the tears fall. I would love to tell Tony how good life is these days, but he knew long before I did.

Miss Hallie, The Original Sweet Southern Woman

A Time to Pray

My mom, Miss Hallie, was almost fifty when my dad died. Because of her cheerful personality, she was a very popular widow. Men followed her around hoping she would go out with them. But she was very selective. In the twenty-three years between her first and second marriage she only dated two men.

A man in our church, Mr. John Melton, who was twenty years older than Miss Hallie, was crazy about her. He sat to the left of the preacher's podium every week, and my mom sat out front with me and my babies. Mr. Melton could not keep his eyes off her.

One Sunday, before the passing of the plate, the preacher called on Mr. Melton to pray over the offering. Mr. Melton was staring at Miss Hallie, oblivious to everyone else, including the preacher. The preacher repeated a little louder, "And now Mr. Melton will lead us in prayer." Mr. Melton didn't even know he was being called on.

After calling on Mr. Melton for the third time the preacher, frustrated by now, yelled, "John! Pray!" Mr. Melton immediately broke into prayer, but he kept one eye open watching Miss Hallie the whole time.

Potted Plants

My Mom, Miss Hallie, had been a widow for almost twenty years when her older sister, Grace, lost her husband. The two sisters decided to drive my Uncle Carson's pickup truck to Florida to visit Grace's daughter, Margie Rae.

The two, both avid gardeners, were admiring Margie Rae's neighbors' plants. She assured them that, although her neighbors were on vacation, they wouldn't mind if Miss Hallie and Aunt Grace took some cuttings to take back to South Carolina.

Several weeks after their return, my mother's nephew, as was his custom, stopped by to have a cup of coffee with her. Miss Hallie was washing the breakfast dishes, and David and I were sitting at the table talking.

Miss Hallie poured David a fresh cup of coffee and while it was cooling he walked over to the old square hot water heater to admire Miss Hallie's assortment of new cuttings. It was full of plants, and he was commenting on them as he looked.

Then he stopped talking. He was staring at one plant with a puzzled look on his face. "Aunt Hallie," he said, pointing his finger at one of the plants, "This is a pot plant."

"Well, yes, it is." Miss Hallie replied. They're all potted right now. I wasn't sure they would grow here, because they're used to a warmer climate. But I'm going to plant them outside as soon as it warms up." She went back to washing dishes.

"Aunt Hallie," he repeated, enunciating each word slowly and distinctly, "This is a pot plant."

Not understanding why he was, once again, stating the obvious, she stopped washing the breakfast dishes and gave him a what-are-you-talking-about look.

Realizing he and his aunt, the widow of a Baptist preacher, weren't on the same page, David spelled it out for her, "Aunt Hallie, it's Marijuana."

She stood there stunned as he finished his coffee, took possession of the potted pot plant, and left with it under his arm.

The moral of the story is this: If you're a little old lady growing pot in your kitchen, don't invite your nephew, the county narcotics officer, over for coffee...

Adults Only

My son, Kevin, had a video store in Waxhaw in the 90's. Instead of an adult section like most stores, Kevin had his adult videos in a room with a door marked private. One day I took Miss Hallie up to see his store. Sure enough, while I was talking to Kevin and his brother Tony at the checkout desk, my little mother found that room.

Now little Miss Hallie loved to snoop, so the word private didn't stop her. I looked toward the back just in time to see her open the door and go in. I nudged Tony and nodded toward the door. Miss Hallie came back out, looking stunned, like she could use a stiff drink......but she didn't drink.

Tony and I stood there, unsure what to do. While we hesitated, Miss Hallie shook her head as if to clear it.

Then she turned around and went back in.

Kevin was dealing with a customer and hadn't noticed. I looked at Tony. He looked at me. We hightailed it out of there, went next door, called Kevin from there and told him where his grandmmother was. After all it was his store.

Quarters

The Alzheimer's that eventually took my mom from us gave random clues before it finally took over. But we missed them because they were brief lapses and scattered far apart. We blamed it on her getting older. It wasn't until she ended up in a town thirty miles away from where she was going that we realized her brain wasn't functioning properly.

Before that happened Miss Hallie frequently took my two younger kids, Aaron and DeAnne and my nephew Josh around town with her when school was out. On these outings, she would stop by where I worked several times during the day, kids in tow.

One day on her third or fourth stop-by, she didn't have the kids with her. "Momma," I asked her, just a little anxious, "Where are the kids?"

She looked around, puzzled, as if she were wondering, too. Then she said, "Oh, I left them at the laundromat."

This time more than a little anxious I told her, "You need to go get them right now. They don't need to be by themselves at the laundromat."

She smiled that sweet Miss Hallie smile and said, "It's okay. I gave them plenty of quarters."

Accidental Flasher

My mom was always funny, and the deeper she settled into Alzheimer's, the funnier she became. I think it was because her normal societal restraints were missing. She would obsess over small things, then move onto something else. For a brief period, her obsession was with women showing bare skin.

Several of the young women in our family were blessed with big boobs. Even with modest tops on, cleavage sometimes showed. And Miss Hallie always pointed it out. One of them was having lunch with us at Bill's BBQ, and Miss Hallie was embarrassing the child with her constant chastisement.

I finally said, "Momma, it's called cleavage." Then, underneath my breath, I added "Oh, you probably don't know what that is anymore."

Miss Hallie, who ordinarily couldn't hear well, heard that, "Yes, I do," she told me. "See." Then she pulled up her blouse. I looked behind me to make sure no one had seen it. There was a man in the booth facing Miss Hallie, frozen in shock.

When I was ushering Miss Hallie out, I glanced at him again. He hadn't moved or closed his mouth. Guess it was the first time he'd been flashed by an 85-year-old.

Funny Little Sinks

Miss Hallie was always a proud little lady. Even after the Alzheimer's had taken over, she didn't like for people to do things for her. She had always been fiercely independent, too, and I could tell it bothered her for me to go into the bathroom with her at Bill's BBQ, our weekly lunch outing place.

Since she had fallen and broken her hip, I didn't like to just leave her to go totally by herself. So, I would hold her hand, walk her to the little hallway leading to the bathrooms and wait in a nearby chair for her to rejoin me.

One Wednesday when I took her hand to walk her to our table, it was really wet. I smiled at her as we walked, a little sadly I admit. Because, although she still remembered to wash her hands, she had forgotten to dry them.

She smiled back with that sweet Miss Hallie smile and said, "I went in the other bathroom this time. They had a funny looking little sink in there. It didn't have a spigot. So, I just washed my hands in the water that was already in the sink."

Fiscally Responsible

My mom, Miss Hallie, still enjoyed Christmas shopping even though she no longer knew what Christmas was. What she enjoyed was the section in Walmart that had dancing, singing Christmas decorations. She would stand there for over an hour pressing the buttons on each one, usually going to another before the previous one had stopped. All the while, smiling with the delight of a small child.

I always waited patiently for her to complete her rounds on our Wednesdays out. My boss understood Wednesdays were long lunches for me, REALLY long. My heart would melt when Miss Hallie would look at me, smile and point to the toy of the moment. I had adapted to the fact that I was now the parent, she the child, and I delighted in her delight.

One Wednesday she was especially taken with a foot tall red and white gorilla. I don't remember the song he sang, but she pressed his button over and over. His being red, her favorite color probably added to her enjoyment.

When I asked if she wanted me to buy it for her, she said, "How much does it cost?" An unusual question because she had forgotten what money was, except for quarters. She recognized quarters because that's what the home she lived in gave to the winners at Bingo and other games the residents played. She used them to buy sodas out of the machines.

I looked at the price tag and told her the gorilla was $18.95. She pressed the button one more time, waited for the song to end, then turned to go. "Don't you want me to buy him?" I asked. She shook her head, sighed and said, "No. That's a lot of quarters."

I Know You

It is 2:05 in the afternoon, and I miss my mom. Just thinking about writing a Mother's Day column has filled me with a nostalgic sadness that puts me into a temporary funk. Yesterday I was good and tonight I'll be fine, but right now it's 2:05 in the afternoon, and I miss my mom.

For the last five years of her life Miss Hallie lived in a nursing home. I drove her there myself from the hospital. The woman who had looked after her children, grandchildren and great-grandchildren was no longer capable of looking after herself.

When we pulled into the parking lot of her new home, she said plaintively, "I thought we were going to Bill's BBQ for lunch". I looked into her sweet, uncomprehending eyes and lied, the first of many I would tell her. I said, "We'll go just as soon as we get you settled."

That pacified her, and by the time we were inside she had already forgotten Bill's BBQ. I signed the papers, stayed with her awhile, went home, and took to my bed for two days. As the years passed, her love remained constant. I felt it every time I was with her. But it had become a generic love, free to all.

I moved to Greensboro in 2010 but still made regular visits to see Miss Hallie. She was always sitting in her wheel chair in the foyer. On my first visit after the move, I walked in, excited, happy, anxious. She looked up at me without a glimmer of recognition and smiled that sweet smile.

My mom had moved from this world, my world, the real world long ago. Her world was inhabited by a husband with no name, children with no gender, and a house with an attic where all her clothes, real and imagined, were stored. Every visit she would ask me to get them. Christians have a mansion in the sky. My mom had an attic.

On this particular day she was incapable of carrying on even a fantasy conversation. Her sentences were random words strung together without meaning. My inability to understand frustrated her. My being there confused her. I was breaking the routine she had grown comfortable with.

So we sat, me reluctant to leave and her not caring either way. My mom was like those dolls from my childhood, programmed to ask questions when you pulled their string, but not programmed to process your answers. She kept asking, "Have you seen my baby?" "My sweet Momma," I yearned to say, "I am your baby."

I got up to leave, and she turned her back on me before I was out of the door. I stood there watching her wheel away, remembering visits to her house before she broke her hip and lost herself in her own mind.

She always followed me to the car with last minute things she had forgotten to tell me or food from the freezer she wanted me to have. All my life she had the solution to every problem I brought her. Just the sight of her made me know everything would be alright.

When you're a writer, the person you most want to impress is your mom or dad. My dad died when I was very young, and for so long it was just my mom and me. I could no longer share my writing with her because Alzheimer's had gained the upper hand.

Although she had gradually forgotten who I was, once in awhile she would say, "I know you. You're Jean Benton." My heart would beat a little faster with joy on the days she told me this.

She fretted over not having a purse, so I took her my Aigner one. It was a gift from an ex. I am not a designer purse kind of woman. I had stocked it with lipstick, fingernail file, hair brush, mirror, and makeup, but she started filling it with a hodgepodge of stuff.

Occasionally, I would go through the bulging purse, sometimes to clean it out so she would have more room for her treasures and sometimes out of curiosity as to what was important to her demented mind.

On one of my cleaning forays, I found a folded clipping from *The Link*, the paper I wrote for. It was one of my columns with my name and picture. It was worn from being opened and refolded, so I knew she was looking at it.

When I showed it to her she turned her head slightly and smiled, childlike. Then she covered that smile with her hand, as if she knew a great secret. After a moment of hesitation, she decided to share that secret with me.

She pointed to the picture from the newspaper, then pointed to me. Still smiling shyly, she proclaimed happily, "I know you. You're Jean Benton".

I was my momma's baby, and I cried like one on the way home that day. I cried because she was so excited to have the woman from the clipping sitting there with her. I cried because she knew I was Jean Benton, but she didn't know that Jean Benton - that I - was her daughter.

Happy Mother's Day, Miss Hallie. Jean Benton loves you...still.

Patience is a Virtue

After Miss Hallie developed Alzheimer's and went to live in the nursing home, I still spent my Wednesdays with her. Lunch and shopping just like we had done for almost twenty years. To keep the confusion minimal, I stuck with the same place for lunch and Walmart for shopping.

But we eventually bought everything red Walmart had to offer, so I one Wednesday I took her to a Family Dollar store. She picked out a few things, and we were in line to pay for them when she discovered the keychain rack on the counter.

Twenty-four keychains with different sayings - four across and six down. She started at the top, read each one aloud...slowly. After each reading she put her hand over her mouth like a child, looked at me, pointed to the keychain and giggled.

I finished paying, but waited for her to finish. The people in line behind us and the cashier were so patient with her, smiling at her enjoyment in such a simple thing. She finally finished. No one let out an audible sigh of relief, but it kind of hung in the air around us.

Then Miss Hallie started over......

The Giggles

My mom, Miss Hallie, a Baptist preacher's widow, was an avid church goer, a tither, ethical, honest, and loved everyone. Not even the smallest bad word ever came out of her mouth. Even when Alzheimer's made her forget not only who I was, but who she was, she kept that same sweet, loving personality.

I used to take her out twice a week. We would have lunch, then go shopping for red stuff, her favorite color. After a couple of years, we had exhausted the bargain stores. We had even managed to buy everything red Walmart had to offer. So, one Sunday I decided to take her to an upscale department store.

I took her in the back entrance to avoid people, but they had just opened, so no customers were in the store. I spied something red on a clearance rack near the front and, holding her hand, walked her slowly toward it.

When we got to it, she looked at the price tag on one of the red tops. Her malfunctioning brain must have taken her back to an earlier time when things cost much less, because she asked in a shocked voice, "Is that how much this cost?" "Yes ma'am," I told her. "It's marked down."

She looked over at the store manager and saleslady standing

nearby and said loudly, "S##t!" This was so far out of character for my sweet little momma that I broke out in a fit of giggles. A look of distaste immediately showed on the sales people's faces.

I decided it might be time to leave, but we had to traverse the entire store.... very slowly. Every few steps, Miss Hallie would, like repeating a mantra, stop and yell s##t back at the man and lady. This made me break out in giggles all over again.

I got her to the back, put her hand on the step rail, told her to stay there and went back to apologize. "I'm sorry," I started, but the look of disdain on their faces made me start laughing again. I repeated, "I'm sorry," and, still laughing, rushed back to Miss Hallie.

As I held the door for us to go through, she turned around and yelled, s##t at them one more time. And, yes, I giggled all the way to the car.

Good Times

My mom, Miss Hallie, and I spent every Wednesday together. At the end of those Wednesdays she always told me, "Well, I had a good time." I continued our Wednesday outings even after she went to live in the nursing home. Until the nursing home asked me not to take her out anymore. The Alzheimer's was so bad, upsetting her routine made her more confused. It was the end of an era for me, very sad.

A year or so later, she had to be taken to the local hospital for a blood transfusion. It was an eight-hour process. She watched calmly as they inserted the needles, but every time they took her blood pressure, she screamed, "Stop, you're killing me!"

My brother, sister and I spent the entire eight hours with her. She alternated between screaming and groaning, not from pain, but from confusion. We tried to sooth her, but to her we were strangers. When it was over three very stressed-out children walked Miss Hallie to my brother's car.

When we had her settled in the car, she looked up at us, smiled that sweet Miss Hallie smile and said, "Well, I had a good time."

A Mother's Love

I repotted a plant I've had for over ten years and found my tiny three-inch brown turtle buried in the dirt underneath the leaves. I sat for several minutes twirling him in my hand as memories sprinkled over my mind like a summer rain.

I was living in Charleston with a sick daughter when I found my little turtle. I thought he was made of wood when I found him in the hospice store in Charleston, but he was heavier and more durable than wood.

My youngest child, DeAnne, was close to death when she was admitted to The Medical University of South Carolina, and I was close to a breakdown. She didn't die. I didn't break down.

After a month of inpatient care, she was transferred to outpatient. She needed treatment five days a week, so I had to move to Charleston temporarily, coming home to work weekends so I could keep my job.

Alone in a strange town for months, teetering on the edge of broke all the time, the Hospice store was our mall. DeAnne always found something in the little store that would bring a brief smile to her face, and that smile would momentarily lift the sadness that had taken root in my heart.

On one of our excursions I found my turtle. I loved turtles and, although I usually didn't spend money on myself, he was only twenty-five cents. I set him on the counter in our pay-by-the-week motel room.

When we came home for good he sat on my dresser to remind me that, like him, I am stronger than I look. When times were better, I placed him in a plant a coworker had given me, and there he stayed for over ten years.

As I twirled the turtle, my thoughts turned from my daughter and me to my own mom. My sojourn in Charleston, as bad as it was, would have been even worse without that little lady. Every weekend when we came home there were two envelopes from Miss Hallie in my mailbox. Mine contained fifteen dollars and DeAnne's contained six dollars.

I know what a sacrifice that money was for my retired mother. She hadn't worked long under Social Security, so only drew about five hundred a month. But, as welcome as it was, the cash was secondary to the love she showered me with.

My mother's love had always been the constant in my ever-changing world. After the divorce, she called long-distance every night to make sure I was home safe before she went to bed herself. It was her love that helped me cope with being the single mother of an ill child, and the financial uncertainty any long illness brings to an already stressed budget.

During the lean years when I could only provide my kids with the basics, she provided the extras - like a new pair of jeans or brand-new jackets to replace the ill-fitting old ones they wore. While I worked two jobs just to feed them, my mom gave us snacks, sodas, and meals out that I couldn't afford.

The years passed. DeAnne got better, and I only had to work one job. Instead of being relieved Miss Hallie worried even more. She became focused on my asthma, afraid I would have an attack while DeAnne was out. She still called long-distance every night and drove up to see me every week.

One night her vigilance saved my life. DeAnne had moved to Columbia to attend college, and I tore my rotator cuff helping her move. The exercises I did to regain the range of movement in my shoulder caused a great deal of pain. Many nights it was unbearable, and pain relievers didn't help.

One night, after several sleepless ones, I was so tired I fell into a deep, dreamless state as soon as I crawled into bed. I don't know how long I lay there before I felt Miss Hallie shaking my uninjured shoulder.

"Jean, wake up, you need to do a breathing treatment," she kept repeating as she gently shook me. She knew nighttime attacks could be very dangerous.

Still, though I heard her and felt the shaking, I was having difficulty responding to her command to wake up. Probably because of the pain pills. Finally, in frustration, she ordered me to get out of bed.

The shaking became extremely vigorous and, in that Momma voice I knew so well, she yelled, "Jean, get up right now! You can't breathe! Get your breathing machine and do a treatment!"

When my usually calm mother yelled, I came fully awake. Miss Hallie was right. I couldn't breathe. I did a breathing treatment like she told me to do. My mother's love for me filled the room as I sat there by myself in the wee hours of the morning breathing the medication in and out.

You see, I was the only one in the house. Miss Hallie was forty miles away in The Chesterfield Convalescent Center. She had been there for two years. By the time DeAnne went away to college I had already lost my sweet momma to the Alzheimer's that had ravaged her brain.

Yet her love for me was such a powerful force it overrode a mind-destroying, memory-destroying disease. On the physical plane she couldn't even remember my name, but when I needed her, she broke through those limits the physical had imposed on her, found me and saved my life.

I love you, Miss Hallie.

I miss you much.

And That's How Traditions Get Started

For as long as I can remember my mom put Poinsettias on graves. I accompanied her on most of these treks. When she was no longer able to drive, I drove her. To Walmart to buy the Poinsettias and to the graves she wanted to place them on.

I never told Miss Hallie, but I don't like Poinsettias. One Christmas a friend, who didn't know about my un-Christmasy attitude toward them, gave me one. I accepted it gracefully-ish and put it in the darkest corner of the living room.

I couldn't bring myself to not water it. Miss Hallie would have been upset with me. But I didn't give it any attention besides the watering. Still it lived and thrived. There in the dark corner of the room.

Unable to tolerate its presence in the house any longer, I put it on the porch. During an ice storm. Plant abuse I know, but I really don't like Poinsettias. By April it was scraggly and ugly, but still living.

Then I remembered all those Christmas Poinsettia runs I had made with my mom. What did it matter that it was April. I put my little orphan Poinsettia in the car, stopped at the first cemetery I saw and placed it on the grave of someone I didn't know.

Sadly, my mom lost the part of her that remembered Poinsettias to Alzheimer's, then lost the battle entirely in 2011. As the disease took over, I chose to continue what she had started. Every Christmas I filled my car with Poinsettias and placed them on graves.

Since 2010 I have been driving down from Greensboro for Miss Hallie's annual Poinsettia run, but I'm getting older. Without even being asked my son Kevin has taken over the Poinsettia tradition. I am hoping when he can no longer do it, one of my grandchildren will take it up.

And one day their children and grandchildren. Then there will come a time when no one will know why they're putting Poinsettias on graves at Christmas. Some will say Great Grandma Jean used to do it, then they'll say Grandpa Kevin always did it.

They won't remember a little lady named Miss Hallie. She will be forgotten. Yet still they will do it because it's a family tradition. And Miss Hallie's Poinsettia runs will go on and on and on and on.

And that's how traditions get started.

Something in Red

My mom, Miss Hallie, loved red. It wasn't an ordinary love. It was a passionate love. And it stayed with her even through the Alzheimer's. My brother, sister and I probably bought her everything red the local stores carried when we took her on day outings from the nursing home.

Once she fell in love with one of those huge stuffed Valentine's Day bears. It was as big as she was, but I bought it for her, had to push her around the store in her wheelchair holding that big red bear with a huge smile on her face.

Miss Hallie left us in 2011. The momma we had known had left a few years before that, but still her death, though not a shock, saddened us deeply. My sister and I went shopping for her burial outfit. We bought a tasteful black suit with just a touch of red in it. We both knew that wouldn't be enough red to satisfy Miss Hallie. Miss Hallie didn't like tasteful. She liked BRIGHT.

When we went to a lingerie store to pick out her undergarments we saw - at the same time - a lacy, sexy fire-engine-red bra. I held it up, looked at Jennie and raised my eyebrows. She smiled and nodded. We knew Miss Hallie would have loved that red bra.

When we took the clothes by, Jenny was upset the funeral makeup didn't totally cover bruises Miss Hallie had sustained from a fall against the bed rails - an accident, no one's fault. I knew Jenny was really upset because our mom had just left us, but she needed to be mad at someone.

I put my hands on her shoulders and said, "Virginia Mae (those of us who have known her since we were knee high to a cotton stalk call her that) you have to calm down. We have a funeral to attend to."

Her eyes were full of tears, but she refused to cry. She said angrily, "But they sent my momma to meet Jesus with bruises on her face."

I looked her in the eye and said, "Virginia Mae, we sent momma to meet Jesus in a red, lacy bra." That did it. I saw the anger dissolve. She smiled as she remembered that moment in the lingerie store when we threw propriety to the wind and bought Miss Hallie something in red.... for the last time.

'Til the End

Except for a photo on the fireplace mantel there are no memories of my Mom in my house here in Greensboro. She has never driven up this driveway, putting on brakes at the last possible moment. Never rushed in this door, ready to leave the minute she got inside, hurrying me to finish dressing so we could go...go...go.

Because of the Alzheimer's, she had already forgotten me by the time I moved here.

In September of 2011, these thoughts caused me to go from room to room conducting a frenzied search for something, anything of my Mom. There was nothing to find, because when I moved to Greensboro, I divided all my keepsakes among my children.

Coming to a stop in my bedroom, I laid both hands on my dresser, closed my eyes, and wept. I wasn't crying because I had nothing that had belonged to my Mom. I was crying because she was leaving us, and we couldn't stop her, couldn't hold her back, couldn't keep her here with us.

Leave us she did, on Saturday morning, September 3, 2011. It was a peaceful passing. Her spirit probably paused a moment to look back at my brother, Julious, who was by her bedside, but the call she had been waiting for had come, and she turned and slipped effortlessly through the veil.

It had been a long wait, and she had become so tired.

The Chesterfield County Convalescent Center was her last abode on the earthly plane, and there, as everywhere, she had touched people with her wonderfully quirky personality. Though Alzheimer's, like a sniper's fire, had ravaged her brain, randomly and slowly, deleting most of her memories, my mother remained a beautiful person until the end.

The woman she had been could still be glimpsed as she scattered love, like graffiti, on everyone who entered the doors of the convalescent center, employees and visitors alike.

My Mom's life was full of hardship and loss, yet she never complained about what she had been handed. Instead she developed the ability to adapt to and even be content in whatever circumstance she was in, whether it was financial, emotional, or physical.

Like her marriage to my father. She married him when she was nineteen, on their second meeting. We weren't privy to why she did such a thing. If you understand the era she was raised in you will know what I mean when I say she talked a lot, but never said anything.

People get married for all sorts of wrong reasons. My dad's wrong reason was obvious. He was a forty-year-old widower with two young children. He needed a wife. I'll never know what my mom's wrong reasons were. She's no longer here to ask.

But I do know my dad was not my mom's forever love. Nor was she his. His heart was with his first wife who died in childbirth. As for my mom, he had never truly captured my her heart. But they stayed together, and she was a faithful wife to him until his death in 1968.

Widowhood suited little Miss Hallie. After my dad's death, she moved from the house they had shared, and her new living room reflected her flamboyant personality. The walls, curtains, cushions, and phone were orange.

There were orange accessories everywhere, and I don't know how she found it, but the carpet was orange. As I shielded my eyes from the glare, she stood there with a proud smile asking me how I liked it.

Miss Hallie lived her life with relish. She never slowed down. There was too much to experience, a new adventure waiting around every corner. She would say, trying to cajole us to join her, "You can go home when you can't go anywhere else."

And she always had a man in her life, even became engaged a time or two. But she remained single for the next twenty-three years, content to live alone. Then at seventy-two my sweet mother met her forever love.

She fell head over heels for Lonnie Perdue. In 1991, only a few months after they started dating, she married for the second and last time.

I had never seen my mom so happy and, in contrast, six months later I had never seen her so sad. Lonnie died on New Year's Eve. When she lost him she was devastated, but she privatized her grief, presented a smile to the world and went on alone.

She went back to her pre-Lonnie life. With one exception. She never dated again. On Monday September 5, 2011, rain fell gently on the tent lending a cadence to Phillip Caulder's words as we laid Miss Hallie to rest beside her forever love, the man she went on loving.... 'till the end.

GOING GRAY

Three Steps Behind

In a less enlightened age, Japanese females were expected to walk three steps behind males as a sign of respect. I grew to womanhood in a household that practiced this archaic attitude. While my Mom didn't walk three steps behind my father physically, her reverence of him was obvious.

They considered it respectful. When I grew old enough to think for myself, I saw it for what it was - subjugating. I was raised in this atmosphere - to be your ordinary butter-melting-in-the-mouth "Rhett, darling, I'm getting the vapors" kind of girl.

However, over the years I discovered I was a different type of Southern woman. I am not a feminist by any means, but I have learned a few things by participating in the give and take, push and pull, tug and shove of the two parties in that continuously swirling eddy called marriage.

When I was young and naïve and even older and naïve, I dove in headfirst without thinking, only to learn I could not keep my head above water in a whirlpool. After trying unsuccessfully to merge my own beliefs with those of another person more than once, I stopped and took inventory.

I concluded that falling in love was easy but climbing back out took a lot of effort. So, I steered clear of love and marriage for over a decade. I had many legitimate excuses for not wanting to get married again.

First and foremost, I didn't think there was a match for me. I wasn't sure if this was because I was too complicated, or marriage was too complicated. I said if I ever even thought of getting married again, he would have to buy a house down the street and call before he came over. I told one woman who was having relationship problems, "Love is like gas – it will pass."

However, as I sat on the bank of the dating pool, occasionally dipping my toes in the muddied waters, I spied a brightly colored stone, standing out from the rest. Much like me, this man had led an eclectic life.

We were so different, yet so much alike. He didn't try to rein me in, smiled at my outrageousness. I knew he was a keeper when I asked to ride the bull at Wal-Mart. He laughed, helped me on and put the fifty cents in. In case you're thinking of doing this, it was very disappointing - not like Urban Cowboy at all.

Yes, after stating unequivocally I would never marry again, I married again. But I am still me. I am stubborn, hardheaded and opinionated. I probably always will be. I do not like losing an argument.

My husband, Doug, and I have heated discussions on politics, religion, and even the origin of words and phrases. We bet quarters on who's right. Just for the record he owes me $7.50. He has learned I will dig in my heels and walk that line until I can't see it anymore.

Still he tries. His latest admonition to me was, "Darling, the dryer is too noisy. I don't want you drying clothes while I'm watching TV. It has to be one of our rules."

Rules indeed. I tilted my head to one side, looked at him with a Karo syrup smile on my face before replying, "Okay, that can be one of our rules."

His smile started slowly because he was amazed at winning that one so easily. Before that smile had time to wrap around his lips, though, I leaned over and turned off the television.

Things Aren't Always What They Seem

When Doug and I started dating, we had a long-distance relationship. I lived in Cheraw, SC, and he lived in Greensboro, NC. It was complicated, but we tried to simplify it as much as possible. We kept clothes and personal items, like hair dryers, toothbrushes and toiletries at each other's houses. That helped us minimize what we had to drag back and forth every weekend.

I overlooked one thing, though – Back scratchers. It's not anything I would have ever thought of. I've never owned a back scratcher. Doug, on the other hand, had one in every room.

This oversight was brought to my attention one weekend when Doug, after taking a shower, said "I think that back-scratcher on your tub drew blood." He turned so I could see. Sure enough, his back was covered in welts and long, open scratches.

Puzzled, I asked, "What back-scratcher? I don't have one. I've never had one."

"Yes, you do," he told me. "I'll show you."

What he showed me was the iron-bristled, long-handled brush I used to clean under the toilet bowl rim. I had apparently laid it on the bathtub when I finished cleaning the commode.

Crackers

When I first started dating Doug, he took me shopping for the perfect pair of cowgirl boots. I had never owned a pair of boots. He was amazed. "If you're going to hang out with the band," he said, "You need cowgirl boots." One of the western stores we visited had quite a few chemicals floating in the air. I have asthma and it's triggered by chemicals.

Now, at that time, Doug was almost perfect...I mean that literally...he had no physical problems of any kind. He seldom went to the doctor, had never been in a hospital and was on no medication of any kind. That is no small feat at our age and something to be proud of. However, it also meant he had no experience in dealing with any type of health problem.

When I started having trouble breathing, he was upset, but very solicitous. He took me out the exit door waving off the protesting clerk, seated me on a bench, almost ran to his car and came back.... with a peanut butter cracker

I also have diabetes and, because we travel with his band on weekends, I keep packs of peanut butter crackers in his glove compartment just in case I need some carbohydrates. I control the diabetes and asthma so well he had never seen me have a problem with either. So, he got the two conditions confused.

While I sat there trying to breathe, he kept saying, "Darling, I wish you would eat this cracker. It'll make you feel better." I didn't have enough air to debate the matter with him, so I waved him off, went to his car and retrieved my rescue inhaler.

After I started breathing again, I ate the cracker, too. Just so I could keep him confused.

Wrong Button

I was sitting with a couple at the band table on a Saturday night not long ago, feeling a tad uncomfortable because I was showing a bit of cleavage. I had taken up the straps on the top that went underneath my blouse, but not quite enough.

Only one thing took the edge off my embarrassment. The attractive lady sitting at the table with me had on a blouse that was much more revealing than mine. She had left a few too many buttons undone, probably purposely. This took the spotlight off me. I knew she was getting more looks than I was.

When the band took a break and the lights were turned up, her husband looked over and said in a peremptory, rather loud tone, "You need to button that thing up. You shouldn't leave it like that."

Although I didn't know them, I felt an affinity with her and made a comment about my own top to show I shared her discomfort. They both looked at me, obviously confused by my remark. Then the husband, realizing I had misunderstood, laughed and pointed to her wallet. It was lying unclasped and open on the table in front of her.

Getting in Shape

My children have noticed my elusive search for the perfect exercise routine. Last year, when my daughter, DeAnne, learned I had canceled my gym membership...again, she bought me a Wii game console and the Wii fit program.

Wii fit is an interactive game that's supposed to make exercising fun. You can march, hula hoop, fly like a bird, ride a bike, even have a snowball fight without moving from your ten by twenty balance board. It is a cornucopia of virtual exercise games.

However, I was working a fulltime job, writing for two papers, and spending my weekends with the band. Exercise wasn't on my schedule, but, because I didn't want to appear ungrateful, I inserted the game disc, entered my information, and custom designed my little avatar - the character representing me in the game world. I even played a few games, but, eventually, after walking around it for two months, I put the balance board back in the box.

Then I moved to Greensboro, got married and stopped working. My son, Aaron, decided it was time to give me another nudge. In December he bought me a new disc for the Wii game. "Mom," he said, "This is great. You don't have to do anything. It has the workout already programmed for you."

His enthusiasm was catching so I opened it, read the instructions, realized I had to enter my weight, and put this one back in the box, too. The Wii balance board weighs you without giving you the option of lying. The only break you get is subtracting the weight of your clothing.

Unfortunately, it has a four-pound clothing weight limit and rejected outright my attempts to enter twenty pounds. I had evaded Doug's questions about my weight for the last two years, and I wasn't about to let this little disc do me in.

One day while Doug was at a recording session, more from guilt than anything else, I loaded the workout program into the Wii. Much to my delight I found I could decline using the balance board, thus making it possible to key in my weight. Of course, I put in a fictitious amount. Good thing, too. Doug checked my info and was amazed at how little I weighed.

First, I built my avatar. There was no short person body, so my avatar's legs are as long as my entire body, and she has a really big bottom, even with the wrong weight. However, I do like her hair. I chose a cute little pixie of a female avatar as my trainer and started my workout. By the end of the half-hour session, I was hot, sweaty and out of breath.

I also found it impossible to get in sync with my avatar. I thought it was her long legs, but after several workouts I realized it was a mirror image thing. Even though my avatar and trainer started everything on the right leg, I was expected to start on my left leg. I suspect this was to get around many humans' inability to recognize left and right when facing someone.

Even with the half hour recovery, and legs so sore I needed to be helped up and down, I felt really good about the whole exercise session, and started on my second day the next afternoon. Five-year-old Landon was visiting, and he wanted to do it. I explained breathlessly - because my avatar and I were running - that it was for adults like me. "Why?" he said innocently, "Is it because you're fat?"

I am now twenty-three days into a thirty-day challenge and, with one exception, I am pleased with the results. The trainer at the bottom of the screen and I had issues, but I shut her up with the mute button. Means I'm flying blind on some of the exercises, but she was just way too irritating.

I have even managed to find a way around my most hated part of the workout - running. It's measured by the nunchuck strapped to your leg. I just take the nunchuck out and shake it up and down. I don't think the trainer expected much of me anyway, because every day there's a note at the end of the workout saying I surpassed her expectations.

Oh, and the one exception I had to this routine: In twenty-three days of exercise, I've gained four pounds. On the other hand, as I run behind my long-legged avatar, I notice she has slimmed down considerably and is developing a really good looking posterior. At least it's working for one of us.

Have You Seen Her?

The band was playing a slow song with a haunting melody. I was absorbed in the music when out of the corner of my eye, I noticed a slim, older gentleman striding purposely across the floor toward the band table. He was shorter than average, but had an air of confidence impossible for a younger man to pull off without appearing arrogant.

His tan pants were of an earlier era, but still not worn in, and the pale blue shirt wasn't colorful enough to attract the eye of would be dance partners. However, his white fedora was. It gave him a jaunty air. Strangely enough he wore slip on sneakers, a bit frayed around the edges. That oddity I understood. With age comes the right to refuse to sacrifice comfort for looks.

His faded blue eyes were smiling, and his teeth weren't store bought as one would expect. If he was nervous it didn't show when he asked me to dance. I usually just line dance, but occasionally, to be polite, I will accept an invitation to dance with a partner, so I smiled and took his hand.

He led me onto the dance floor, explaining as we walked how new he was to all of this. While we danced he told me of his wife's passing and how alone he was. He had started taking dance classes at the senior center the year before to assuage the loneliness, and found he had a knack for it. He asked how often I came to this particular place. I told him the steel guitar player was my boyfriend, so I would always be there when this band performed.

He rambled on, continuously complimenting me, and I got a been here before feeling. Single women hear a variety of pick-up lines, and my dance partner, despite his age, seemed very adept at small talk. I mentally chided myself. Eighty-four was a bit old to be picking up women, especially one young enough to be a daughter.

After the dance ended, he kept me on the floor waiting for the next song. It was an infectious fast-paced one, and I was concerned he wouldn't be able to keep up. Much to my surprise he almost out-danced me...almost. I had a thoroughly enjoyable time dancing with this engaging man. At the end of the night he came to my table, coat draped over his arm, and asked if I would favor him with one last dance before he left.

Two months later I returned with the band, and much to my surprise he was there. I smiled when I saw him, but he didn't return my smile. He looked agitated as he circled the floor moving between the dancing couples, his eyes surveying the room. It was obvious he was searching for someone. I stood up as he approached the band table, ready to hit the dance floor, but he was clearly preoccupied.

"Have you seen her?" he asked.

Seeing my puzzled look, he elaborated, "She said the guitar player was her boy, and she traveled around with the band. I have looked everywhere for her, but I can't find her."

I laughed, "That was me. The steel guitar player is my boyfriend, not my boy."

He scrutinized my face and hair, which was shorter, curlier, and a different color... I am, after all, a woman...before replying, "No, you're not her. There was something very special about this woman. I really liked dancing with her, and she promised we would dance again when this band came back. But I can't find her."

After doing another sweep of the room without finding the absent me, he decided to while away the hours by dancing with the present me, and the other women at our table. At one point, in an attempt to prove my identity, I gave him a recap of that night two months before, complete with the coat over the arm ending.

"Yes," he said, unable to contain his excitement, "That was her. Is she here. Have you seen her?"

I gave up and just chitchatted with him as we danced. When the band members took a break, he questioned them about the guitar player's mother. No one could enlighten him. They were totally puzzled by this phantom woman he described. At the end of the evening, he asked me to tell me hello if I saw me. I assured him I would.

Last week he came to another place the band was playing, but this time I was prepared. I pretended I wasn't me and smiled politely at him when he came over. He smiled even bigger than I did, took my hand and said excitedly, "There you are. I missed you last time. Did that lady tell you I said hello?"

Looks Familiar - Hum a Few Bars

The first year Doug and I were married, I attended a lot of Christmas parties with him. He plays in a band, The Delmonicos, and December is full of events for a dance band. The average woman only has so many red outfits in her closet, and I had run out of Christmas-y clothes.

I didn't want to buy something to wear just for Christmas, so on gig night I was looking through my closet, trying to come up with something festive. I saw the burgundy top I had worn for my wedding hanging in the back of the closet. Happy, I pulled it out and put it on.

When I walked into the living room Doug's eyes lit up. He said, "That is a beautiful top. Why haven't you worn it before. Or is it new?"

My husband hadn't remembered what I wore when we got married. I could get a lot of mileage out of that one. I savored the moment for a few minutes before finally telling him.

He was unfazed, said, "Well you only wore it once. If you had worn it more often I would have recognized it."

Einstein He Ain't

After Doug and I married, I was combining our bookshelves. Marrying a man who had bookshelves that contained books he had actually read was wonderful. As I was going through them, I came across one written by Albert Einstein. It was apparently signed by the author. The inscription read "Doug, you are a smart kid. Grow up strong. Al."

"Where did you get this?" I asked speculatively. A book signed by Albert Einstein himself would certainly be a collector's item, but that it was signed to Doug made it questionable.

My new husband didn't hesitate, which made me realize he wasn't a novice at the BS stuff. Without blinking an eye, he said, "Neat, isn't it? My class went on a field trip to The Smithsonian when I was in elementary school, and he was there. I bought the book and he signed it for me."

He was so believable. Had I been anyone but me, I might have believed him. But, nope...I didn't believe him.

"Darlin'," I said in a voice dripping with sarcasm. "Didn't Albert Einstein die about the same time you were born?"

"Man," he said. "It's heck being married to a smart woman."

Directionally Challenged

I don't have GPS, OnStar or a TomTom. They irritate me. I use pen and paper and write out extremely specific directions when I'm traveling to a new place. Still, it very seldom turns out well for me. I learned years ago to add getting-lost-time to the time Google maps tells me it will take to reach my destination.

When I first moved to Greensboro, going anywhere was like stumbling around in the dark feeling for a light switch. One Sunday I went two miles down the road to get burgers. The trip back took forty miles. Doug could not understand how I got lost driving to Burger King.

Full disclosure takes a lot of time when you're my age, so I had not yet communicated my problems with North, South, East, and West to Doug. After my Burger King trip, I had to sit down with him and explain that, of course, I got lost. It's what I do.

In the 8 years I've lived here, I have been lost in Thomasville, Greensboro, High Point, Lexington, Trinity, Winston Salem, and Archdale several times. I have wandered into a few other towns, but can't say I got lost in them. I was already lost when I got there. I eventually found my way out.

Doug knows the towns around Greensboro very well, but he is of no help to me. The man has a problem with communicating verbal directions. He'll say Highway 62 when he means Highway 68, Exit 64 when he means Exit 96 will take you to Highway 64.

He told me a shortcut to my daughter's apartment complex that incorporated back roads.   The fourteen-mile trip back took thirty-two miles because he told me to turn left when I should have turned right.

Last year I gained some valuable insight into directions. Doug sold a house and financed it for the buyer. While Doug was doing his daily walk, the guy, a carpenter, called to say he was working near us. He wanted to know if Doug could run over and pick up the house payment.

I wrote down the directions to give Doug - Go through Pleasant Garden. Get over on 22, and take a right at the Get 'N Go. He would be exactly 5 miles down that road, on the right across from a generator business. His work van and truck would be in the driveway.

Doug read my directions. "What does get over on mean?" he asked skeptically.

"It's Southern for get on. Just leave out the word over and read it as get on 22," I informed him.

"I can't understand a word of this," he told me, shaking my directions at me. "I'm going to have to call him back."

Doug's end of the phone conversation went like this - "So I get on 22 and turn right at the gas station. Uh-huh. Exactly five miles. Uh-huh. Across from the generator business. Uh-huh. What do I look for? Your van and truck. Uh-huh. Okay, I've got it now."

Finally, I understood. All my years of frustration with directions could have been avoided if I had just known the importance of the uh-huhs.

Clocks

I had not planned on retiring when I moved to Greensboro. As a single mom, I had worked two jobs when my kids were young, then worked and gone to school when they were older. For someone raised with a strong work ethic, the thought of doing nothing at all seemed to border on decadence.

I had also lived alone for over a decade and spending that do-nothing time with another person made me a bit apprehensive. Doug, my new husband, insisted I at least give it a try. He played in a band on weekends and didn't want a job to keep me from traveling with him.

At first, I felt guilty about staying up as late as I wanted and sleeping until I woke up, but I adapted quickly to my husband's lifestyle. It wasn't long before I put the alarm clock in a box with some other things and stored it in the utility room.

After a couple of years, Doug found the box while searching for acrylic paint. Delighted, he came into the living room where I was watching TV and held the alarm clock up for me to see.

"Look what I found," he said with a big grin. "I'm going to set it. What time do you want to get up?"

"Why in the world do you want to do that?" I asked.

"Just for fun," he said, "Come on. Give me a time."

"Okay," I relented, deciding to humor him. "Set it for 9:30, put it on your side of the bed, turn it off when it alarms, and let me sleep another half hour."

This satisfied him, and he went to bed. A couple of hours later, I was still up, watching a rerun of Perry Mason. He came in the living room, squinted his eyes at me and said in a sleepy voice, "Darling, you need to come to bed. You have to get up at 9:30."

Just a Couple of Bohemians

I moved to Greensboro with the intention of continuing the lifestyle I had in Cheraw. I would find a forty-hour job, continue my feature writing, and branch out into fiction. However, I did not realize how seductive the Bohemian way of life can be.

Doug and I aren't total Bohemians. Early Bohemians were musicians, writers, and artists living nontraditional lifestyles as do we, but they also were transients who chose a life bordering on poverty to live the way they wanted.

Doug and I live without what some people consider necessities, such as dish network, but we aren't as impoverished as the early Bohemians, and, while traveling around with a band might seem transient, we have a home base to go back to.

Other than that, we fit the description of Bohemian perfectly. Our lifestyle is not a traditional one, we don't work nine to five jobs, and we're not in line with the views of mainstream society on many issues.

While Doug fits comfortably into mainstream politics, my political views might be considered unorthodox by some. That is if people knew what they were. After two years of being married, Doug is still not sure what political party I'm registered with.

Our lifestyle reminds me of the simplicity of my growing up years, when there were fewer grey areas, and the different shades of black and white were easier to discern. Back when we had values that were set in stone by those who lived before us, and we knew exactly what we believed in.

As for physical needs, we had a roof that only leaked during extremely heavy downpours - aluminum pots took care of that - heat in the winter with wood we cut ourselves and natural foods from our own little piece of earth. We didn't even know what a snack was, but looking at the shape we're in from snacks makes me think that wasn't a bad thing.

My family's first television set was a black and white one my sister purchased with the earnings from her first job. We received three channels, one clear and the other two different shades of fuzzy. On a good reception day, we could almost get a fourth one. We just had to make up our own story line to go with the random bits of video and audio we glimpsed.

To channel surf, we had to sit on the floor by the TV while manually changing channels, and only having three channels made it an extremely short surf. The free antenna TV we have now is a big step up from those days, but some would see it as deprivation. Where do people find the time to watch over a hundred channels anyway?

Even though Doug and I share the same basic values with just enough differences to add spice to the relationship, my life underwent a complete overhaul after the move. Of course, when he looked around his house after I was done with it, I guess you could say his did, too.

He did manage to keep the wood and brass table lamp which is almost as tall as I am and does not deserve to be called a table lamp. There isn't a table in the house that can hold it. It's not that I didn't try to get rid of it. I put it with the goodwill items three times and sent it home with his son twice.

When I started on the music room which was painted in varying shades of purple, I found it hidden behind an amp. With a sigh of resignation, I set it on the piano. A man has needs, and Doug needed that lamp. What he didn't need was a purple music room. Marriage is about compromise, after all.

When it comes to furnishings, I delight in functional, but Doug has his own views on functional. His couch was positioned to within a couple of feet of his big screen TV, which made the room decidedly off-center.

He agreed to move it back against the wall with the stipulation that it be returned to its original place during football season. I smiled and nodded, knowing full well that wasn't going to happen.

I am gradually buying into Doug's way of life. I am learning to sit in the sun more and on the couch less. He has taught me that life is more enjoyable without many of the encumbrances that society thinks we can't live without.

There are those who say I have dropped out of life. I would argue that point. I think I am just now discovering it.

Light, Water and Love

I am a lover of plants. My husband Doug is a lover of plants. We just love them differently. I love the way they add to the looks of a room. I don't think a room is complete without a plant in it. I place them esthetically, water them as needed, and prune them occasionally.

Doug, on the other hand, treats them as if they were his children. He sprays them on a regular basis, rubs dust off their leaves, puts them outside on pretty days, feeds them on a fixed schedule, and places them where each individual plant will get just the right amount of light.

I am not really surprised at this high level of care the Palmer plants receive. Doug treats the dog and me the same way. Well, maybe the dog gets a little more personal attention than I do. When I pointed this out to Doug, he asked if I wanted him to scratch my belly and let me sleep on his dirty underwear beside the bed.

Doug taking over the care of my plants when we married wasn't a bad thing. I do remember the tendril of one plant in my dining room always lying across the floor waiting to grab my leg and beg for water.

However, his taking over was based on the misconception that I had neglected them. Always highly observant, he noticed on our first date that two of the prettiest planters in my living room held dead plants.

What he had no way of knowing, because I don't share everything on first dates, was they had been dead for over two years. I had indeed neglected them when I was dating someone else, but by the time Doug came along I had mended my ways.

I kept the poor dead things as a reminder that a man is never worth losing a plant over. First impressions are important, though, and Doug had pegged me as a bad plant owner. After that first date he couldn't wait to get his hands on my.... plants.

As proof of my ability to take care of growing things, I reminded Doug of my eleven-year-old corn plant. It was only about four inches high when a friend gave it to me, and it's grown into a beautiful four-foot tall specimen of plant hardiness.

Can you believe he took the credit for that, said it was because he had repotted it. Now I bought that pot at Lowe's before I met him, so being an experienced wife, I didn't hesitate to accuse him of lying like a dog.

He qualified his original statement by saying he had taken it out, shaken the dirt off the roots and put new dirt in the pot. I am sure you will agree with me that re-dirting and repotting are two different things.

Either way, I no longer have to look after the plants. They're on the front porch, the deck, the side yard getting just the right amount of love, light and water. The plants like our dog and all the other animals that inhabit the Palmer Estate are pampered beyond belief.

And if I ever feel the need of a little extra attention myself, I just scratch Doug's foot and bark.

Jean and the Super Star

Last week my new husband cooked breakfast for us. I offered to do the grits, but he turned me down. "I am a Southern girl," I told him. "I know how to cook grits." He still turned me down. I left him to it and went in the music room to work on an article.

The smell of bacon frying was a nice accompaniment to my typing, but when he brought my plate, it was clear he should have accepted my offer. The grits looked like grainy marshmallows. He followed my gaze to the large clumps and said with an apologetic grin, "They are a little chewy."

After the breakfast debacle we decided to have lunch out. When I pulled my unwashed hair back with mismatched combs, I noticed the grey streaks shining at the temples. I shrugged it off just as I had dismissed the yellow mustard stain on my light blue sweater.

After all, I wasn't going to see anyone I knew. While I often long for the friendliness of my small hometown, I do enjoy the anonymity of this big city. I slid my feet into slippers without socks and hopped in the car.

Cracker Barrel was crowded. As we worked our way to the middle dining area, a man cupped his hands around his mouth megaphone style and yelled, "Doug Palmer, you are wanted at this table." Doug turned toward the sound of the voice while I, thinking it was one of his musician friends, continued following the hostess to our table.

The hostess seated us one table over from Doug's friend. Before I could sit down Doug waved me over. I scanned the faces at the table and, and realizing this was a family event, smiled at the group before turning to be introduced to megaphone man.

My first thought was how extremely nice looking he was. Yes, guys, we notice things like that, too. We're just more discreet with it than you. The thought that followed was, "I've seen this man before."

Then Doug said, "Crash, this is my wife, Jean. Darling, I'd like you to meet Crash Craddock."

Billy "Crash" Craddock, the King of Country Rock, the man who brought sexy to country music, charted twenty top ten singles, appeared on countless television shows, and played to audiences all over the United States and world reached for my hand.

When I was fifteen I took my niece to use the restroom in the old Chesterfield County Courthouse. I had giant tin can curlers in my hair, pants I had made into shorts with pinking shears, and was barefoot.

While we were in the restroom, my state's United States Senator had set up for a stump meeting in front of the courthouse. I had to push through the town dignitaries to get back to the car.

As I hurried by him, toddler on my hip and head down, the politician grabbed my hand and shook it. When Billy "Crash" Cradock, Super Star, reached for my hand I was fifteen again with curlers in my hair and no shoes.

Doug was totally at ease in his knock-around jeans and tie-dyed T-shirt but as one of Crash's original Dream Lovers, he had spent almost a decade touring and recording with the guy. When you share a bathroom on a bus for that long you become very comfortable with one another.

Well, two buses. Crash sold the first one because Doug threw up on one of the mattresses...the things I learned that day. On the other hand, my in-need-of-a-dye-job hair, stained sweater and sockless feet were making me uncharacteristically shy.

Crash and I chatted for awhile. He was very gracious, just a regular guy. He and Doug went on talking about the old days, and I returned to our table. When Doug joined me, the conversation continued across the tables. Crash told me about some of the tricks Doug had pulled at concerts and on the bus.

Then, out of the blue, Doug said, "Crash, Jean writes for a paper up here. You should let her interview you."

"We can do that," Crash replied. Smiling at me he recited his cell phone number. "Just give me a call, and we'll set it up."

As I keyed the in the number, the young me who had watched him on TV back in the day was jumping up and down chanting, "I have Billy Crash Craddock's cell phone number. I have Billy Crash Craddock's cell phone number", while the old woman me calmly thanked him and nodded acquiescence.

I haven't called to schedule the interview, yet. For now, it is enough to just look in my contacts and see the cell phone number of The King of Country Rock. What are the odds a trip to Cracker Barrel on a Sunday afternoon would bring you up close and personal with someone whose records you bought as a young woman?

While I waited for our order I sent this text to my friend, Barbara, a cardiac nurse: "Billy "Crash" Craddock just shook my hand. Should I wash it?"

Her reply was immediate, reflecting her years of nursing experience, "Only if he has a cough or is vomiting." Girlfriends keep it real for you, don't they?

Bargain Basement

While I was dating Doug and for several years after we were married, we were stalked by a group of really silly women. One of them had dated him briefly before I met him, and she played the part of scorned woman to the hilt. Inexplicably, her friends joined her in her hate campaign. I won't go into detail, but they did everything under the sun to harass us, some of it strange indeed.

We ignored everything they did, no need to fuel the fire. But one night we came home to a message on our answering machine complaining because Doug had let me wear his jacket at an outdoor show he played. Yep, they were upset I was wearing my husband's jacket.

I was amazed at the anger in the message. I told my new husband I was used to being liked, that I had never been hated until I met him.

He held his hands out and said jokingly, "Darlin', what can I say? That's just the price you pay for being Mrs. Doug Palmer."

I looked him up and down, shook my head, and told him, "I think I was overcharged."

Coexisting

The fact that Doug was from Tennessee was a big plus in my decision to date him. He couldn't possibly be related to anyone I had dated, married, hung out with, or passed on the street. I knew he had an ex-wife, but they had been divorced for years, so I was confident she wouldn't be a problem.

I am not sure exactly how long we had been dating when I learned his ex-wife and her husband lived next door. I remained calm on the outside when he told me, but mentally I was slapping myself upside the head.

Doug explained she had asked for the place next door in the divorce, even though he had offered her another house in a different town. He said he had no idea why she didn't take the other house. Yes, he's really that naïve.

Now, I know what you're thinking. You're thinking I'm a saint, because only a saint could live next door to her new husband's old wife. Okay, maybe that wasn't what you were thinking. Despite numerous and at times strange attempts to get Doug's attention, I did fine for the first few months after I moved in.

Then the old wife's new husband decided we weren't giving him the proper respect by still using the circle driveway. The property line went through the middle of it. One day he spent hours putting logs the size of light poles across the paved driveway, blocking us from using it. Still, our house was paid for and it was a bad time to sell. So, we just started backing out of our driveway.

Most of the time I shook my head and smiled at their silliness. I was even nice the day she came rushing in our back door without knocking. She was supposed to pick their grandson up at an address she wasn't familiar with. She was upset she was going to be late and came to see if Doug knew where the street was.

Doug had no idea and, since she didn't have a computer or GPS, he told her I would map quest it for her. She sat on the couch beside me while I opened my laptop and looked up the address.

Even though I knew the boobs pushing against my shoulder weren't real - Doug had told me how much they cost him - it was still an awkward situation. But I handled the situation with as much grace as I could muster. I brushed her hair out of my face, found the place and wrote the address down for her. She thanked me profusely, thanked Doug even more profusely and left.

With every new attempt she made to get his attention, Doug told me to bide my time. They were both smokers, and we would probably outlive them. However, one day I walked out of our back door and there she was. Reclining on the pavement on her side of the circular driveway beside the logs. She looked like Burt Reynolds in Cosmopolitan. I knew I had to do something.

And so, the holidays are here. It's the season for being thankful. Every time I step out into my yard, I am thankful for that eight-foot privacy fence I had installed last month. I don't know if Robert Frost was right when he said good fences make good neighbors. What I do know is if you build that fence high enough and long enough it makes coexisting way more tolerable.

Nice Try

Doug and I bought new bunk beds for the grandkid bedroom. We put the beds together ourselves. I did the instruction reading because men think they're born knowing how to put stuff together, so they don't need instructions

Doug looked up from the floor where he was connecting slats and asked how much weight the bottom bunk would hold. It was a full bed while the top was a single. I was concentrating on the instructions, so replied rather absently, "Three hundred pounds".

I was absorbed in the paper in front of me and failed to realize where he was going with that question. For years he has been trying to trick me into telling him how much I weigh. He even sneaked a look at my SC driver's license. It said 135 lb. I was good with that.

"Then we can sleep on it together, right?" I looked down at him. He was grinning. He repeated, "Right?" I looked at the bed slat in my hand, sighed and put it down to remove temptation. Guess I'll sleep on the new bed with him to throw him off, but I'll be holding my breath the entire time.

Douglas Scissorhands

I have kind hair. I suspect most of you are from the South, but if you aren't, that is an old descriptive, derogatory phrase for unmanageable hair. My hair is neither curly nor straight, and it's so thick that no amount of layering can thin it out. I became resigned to this long ago and just rope it in when it gets too "kind".

Doug, on the other hand, has only known me for a couple of years, and he has trouble accepting this. He thought I just needed the right beautician. Three beauticians later, my hair looked the same. He decided it was up to him do what the experts could not – tame my hair.

When he asked if I would let him cut and thin my hair, I smashed his visions of making me the next Farrah Fawcett by turning him down cold. He countered with, "Darling, I'm an artist." It is true that in addition to being a very talented musician, he also paints. Plebian that I am, I could not grasp a connection between my hair and his painting.

I have always believed we learn by doing and, often times, we learn by doing it wrong. It was time for Doug to learn that hair is a whole new ball game, and there is a reason beauticians go to cosmetology school.

Last week I handed Douglas Scissorhands the hair cutting tools.

He took them hesitantly, looking for a catch, but I sat calmly down in the chair and waited for him to begin. When he realized I was serious he smiled and set to work with a vengeance.

He used the thinners first. My calmness turned to apprehension as I watched chunks of my hair drop to the floor. Remembering this was a teaching experience, I kept my mouth shut - a very difficult thing for me to do. When my new stylist had trimmed and thinned my hair to his satisfaction, he reached for the shaver. Apprehension turned to dread.

"What are you going to do with that?" I asked fearfully.

"I'm going to shave your neck," he said cheerfully, obviously pleased with his work.

"But you didn't cut my hair short enough to shave my neck," I protested.

"It'll make you cooler," he countered, coming toward me with shaver humming.

Good sense kicked in and, scissors in hand, I threatened him with bodily harm if he didn't drop the shaver. Hair Cutting 101 was over. I looked in the mirror. I didn't have much hair anymore – he really liked the thinner shears - and what I did have was considerably shorter.

My hair turned under, it turned up, it stuck out, and some sections were shorter than others. I reserved judgment until I washed and dried it. Then I freaked out.

"I look like a fifties housewife, only in color," I moaned.

Now, had I been thinking rationally, I would have done this on a Monday. As it was I only had an hour to get ready for the dance his band was playing that night. I did what I could and thanked the stars above for low lighting. Doug spent the forty-five-minute drive to the gig turning my mirrored visor back up every time I turned it down.

"My hair looks horrible," I complained.

"It's because you aren't smiling," he explained. "Frowning makes your hair look bad".

It is impossible to explain Doug's logic, but he sounded very sincere. When we arrived the band members, after their initial shock wore off, commiserated with me. The drummer tried to cheer me up by pointing out I had achieved a retro look.

"Kind of like the fifties?" I asked.

"Yeah, "he said, "That's it. Looks exactly like the fifties."

I gave Douglas Scissorhands my best "I told you so" glare. He ignored me. I realized he had decided on a strategy for dealing with the hair cutting debacle. He was going to ignore it. I guess it'll be a month or two before he looks at my head again.

Eventually my hair will grow back. All is not lost, because Doug learned a valuable lesson. or did he? He had sworn he would never take scissors to my hair again, but when the band went on break, Nancy, one of the singers, told me I should get highlights while I let it grow out. She thought that would detract from the raggedy appearance.

Doug, who had been watching the line dancers, perked up at this suggestion.

"Highlights", he said, turning to Nancy. "I can do that."

"Have you ever done it before?' Nancy queried, looking at him incredulously.

"Well, no" he said reluctantly, "but I've seen it done. It doesn't look too hard."

Hair Styling 102 will have a different teacher. This one has retired from the adult education program.

Old Dogs and Children

Unconditional loyalty is rare, but there are two exceptions - old dogs and little children. Once you gain the loyalty of either, you can do no wrong in their eyes. They will defend you to the moon and back, even if it means physically jumping on your attacker.

When I married Doug, he had three of these defenders in his life - Buddy and Precious, his Jack Russell Terriers and Landon, his only grandson. Buddy and Precious had lived in style in the basement for over a decade. Their world was replete with indoor and outdoor dog houses, and a doggie door leading to a large fenced-in back yard.

Doug's steel guitar repair shop was in the basement, so they received constant attention. Three times a week Buddy got a new toy, and Precious, who stuck her nose up at toys, got specialty bread from restaurants we visited. Doug even buttered it for her.

Precious ruled the basement, making Buddy wait until she had checked out both food bowls before he could eat, snapping at him if he made a move before she gave the go-ahead. They were like an old married couple, and Doug was the son they both idolized.

Buddy was already in his dotage when I moved in. I don't know if it was age or his relationship with Precious that made him ornery. Either way, he made it clear another woman would not be welcome in his life.

I decided not to push the envelope and left him alone. He passed away not long after I met him, and I was glad I had not butted in on his relationship with Doug. After he died, Precious lived up to her name, displaying the sweetness that had earned her that name in the first place.

She graciously allows me to pet and feed her, but her gentleness doesn't fool me. I know if she could, she would slam the door behind me and lock it every time I go outside.

On the other hand, she whines when Doug leaves and cries outright when he pets the neighboring dogs that wander into our yard. This happens a lot. Word has spread there's a pushover at the Palmer residence.

Winning Landon over fell somewhere between Buddy's orneriness and Precious' snobbery. He was not used to sharing his Papaw time. Added to that, a woman Doug dated before me still baby sits him. Over five years later, still angry at being rejected, she uses her time with Landon to fill him with false information.

In the beginning my conversations with Landon were full of she saids.

Landon: She said you married Papaw for his money.

Me: Nope. Papaw married me for my money. I'm rich. (I firmly believe it is okay to lie to your children and grandchildren if it's for a good cause.)

Landon: For real?

Me: Yep, ask Papaw

Landon: Can we go to Wal-Mart and get a toy?

Most of my counters worked. Eventually, he went from tolerating me to accepting me. Of course, his loyalty still lies with Papaw, but mine does, too, so we're good. Thankfully, we finally had our last "she said" conversation.

Landon: She said you were fat.

Me: She has never seen me.

Landon: Seriously?

Me: Yep. She lives 100 miles from here, and we've never met.

Landon: Then how did she know you were fat?

Sigh.... Thank goodness Precious can't talk.

Me, Me, Me

To be so talented, Doug is not into himself, and he recognizes the focus is on him in most of the places we go. People love musicians anyway, but he was one of the original Dream Lovers and they like talking to someone they still see on RFD TV occasionally.

I don't mind any of this. I'm very secure in my husband's feelings for me as well as my own abilities. I have my own fan base because of my writing, so I'm content to let him shine at the dances. But, randomly, the fact that I left my life in South Carolina to join him in his world makes him feel a bit guilty, and he tries to make up for it.

Not long ago, as I was leaving to go shopping, he took both of my hands in his, looked into my eyes and told me he realized it had been all about him since we had gotten married.

"I'm going to do something about that," he said in his most sincere voice. "When you get back this afternoon, I'm taking you to Cracker Barrel. It's Monday and they have those grilled pork chops I really like."

Keeping up with the Kardashians

A few years ago, Doug was filling in with a band that had a look-at-me girl singer. She tended to dress a little outrageously, the flashier the better. Her makeup was over the top, too. One night she wore a dress that was probably tighter than her skin.

She was a pretty girl with a nice figure, but this night her butt was extraordinarily big. In fact, it was sticking out like Kim Kardashian's. Those of us who knew her were speculating out loud if it was just the tightness of the dress or did she had on one of those fake butts.

Doug, who was on break, listened to us go back and forth about it without commenting. Then he went back on stage where the girl singer was looking at the set list. He leaned over her shoulder, pointed to the paper, and asked her something. She nodded her head, and he came back to the table.

"It's fake," he told us when he sat back down.

"How do you know?" several of us asked almost in unison.

" 'Cause I pinched it really hard," he told us, "And she didn't even flinch."

Date Night

My husband Doug plays steel guitar and tenor saxophone with a popular band, so my weekends are filled with friends, fun and dancing. However, he's on stage working, so, I spend very little time with him at the venues they play.

A couple of weeks ago, in addition to performing four nights in one week, he also rebuilt a vintage steel guitar for a customer. On Wednesday he said, "Darling, I've missed you. We need some quality time. Get dressed up. I'm taking you to a nice restaurant." I had been missing him, too, so I was excited about having a date night with my husband.

We drove to a nearby town, had a delicious meal, quiet conversation, and by the end of the evening we were back in sync. As soon as we arrived home, though, Doug said he wasn't feeling well and went straight to bed. I was going to join him, but I started feeling sick, too.

By midnight we were playing musical chairs with the bathroom. Food poisoning? A virus? We didn't know. But our date night had gotten seriously off track. At some point during that never-ending night, Doug started feeling extreme pain in his side. I thought he had pulled a muscle from heaving, but he wasn't so sure.

When daylight came he had me tell the band he wouldn't be able to play that night. Forty years of performing and this was the first time he had missed a show. I took him to the emergency room. Several hours later, after scads of blood work and a CT scan, we had a diagnosis. Doug's appendix had ruptured. Emergency surgery was going to top off our date night.

The surgeon explained what would happen during and after the surgery, showed Doug the places on his abdomen where he would be cut. I blame the morphine shot for Doug's reaction to that information. He looked over at me and said with a catch in his voice, "Darling, they're going to ruin my perfect body."

Doug had never been in a hospital or had surgery. But this wasn't my first rodeo. I knew those little scars were going to be the least of his worries, but I thought he would do better on a need to know plan instead of a full disclosure one.

"The scars won't be so bad," I reassured him. "You can even cover them with a tattoo if they bother you - maybe a cute little pink rose." I was hoping my chatter would divert him from the IV needle they were trying to insert. He won't even let me use a sewing needle to take a splinter out, so I didn't want him to get a good look at that one.

My tattoo suggestion didn't reassure him. Off he went to surgery focused on scars, and off I went to the waiting room focused on Doug. By the time the operation was over, I had set up camp in his room and was in full blown nurturing mode, a side to me he had never seen.

For several days Doug malingered, not wanting to face the world outside his hospital room. He had banned visitors, even family, and asked that I keep the room darkening blind closed all the time.

Then one morning he got out of bed and told me, "Open that blind and put on my robe so we can go walking. I'm through being sick."

Elated, I had the robe in my hand when his nurse knocked on the door and said, "Mr. Palmer, the doctor told me to give you a suppository to make your bowels move." I laid the robe down, and he climbed back into bed.

The two of us settled into hospital life. He would watch TV while I sat in a chair beside his bed doing crossword puzzles. Occasionally we would go walking down the halls - he in his robe and me in his pajamas. I had to hold the pajamas up, because Doug's legs are about two feet longer than mine.

Doug's hospital bed wasn't big enough for both of us, so I had to make do with the plastic couch under his window. I did not sleep well on it for several reasons, the foremost being worry for my sick husband.

The night before he was discharged I was so tired I fell into a deep sleep. I awoke with a jerk after an hour and a half. Feeling guilty for dozing off like that, I tiptoed over to check on my sick husband.

The spread which had been across the bottom of his bed was his only cover. His blanket was missing. Puzzled, but not wanting to disturb his sleep looking for the blanket, I went back to my hard-as-a-rock couch. Picking up my own blanket to straighten it before lying back down, I found I now had two.

While I was sleeping, Doug had gotten out of bed, unplugged his IV, and pulled it across the room so he could lay his blanket over me. With tears running down my face, I returned his blanket to his sleeping body. I went back to my makeshift bed, no longer wrapped in his blanket, but still wrapped in his love. I'm thinking maybe we didn't need a date night after all.

Art of Distraction

I used to think my husband Doug was a novice at the art of distraction. When he had surgery, I brought him home from the hospital, settled him in bed and told him to knock on the wall if he needed anything. Six knocks and thirty-minutes later, I pushed the door open - a little harder than necessary - and went stomping in.

I had only gotten a few frustrated words out when he looked into my eyes and said, very sincerely, "You look beautiful today." Then he added, "Would you mind handing me the back scratcher?"

I had on bright red pajama bottoms decorated with black and white polar bears, a man's size 4X burgundy t-shirt which came to my knees and could have held a couple of more people, pink fluffy bedroom shoes and his navy robe, which was too long and too big. My hair was in a bun on top of my head.

Doug's attempt to distract me with flattery was so outrageous, I shut up, handed him the back scratcher, and left the room. I knew I had been wrong in categorizing him as a novice in the art of distraction. I was dealing with a pro.

The Importance of Drawing Water

It was instilled in me as a child to draw water when it was going to snow, sleet or if temperatures would be dropping extremely low. This was in the days of inadequate insulation and freezing pipes. I haven't had a frozen pipe in decades, so I've conditioned myself not to worry about temperatures in the teens. However, when it's going to snow or sleet, I still draw water.

On the other hand, the news stations didn't try to make the weather such a dramatic thing when I was a child. Now they build it up for days. Half a dozen times already this winter I've drawn a bathtub full of water, and filled every pot, pitcher and jug in the house, only to pour it all out the next day. Last week we had still another warning. Fed up, I ignored it.

I shouldn't have.

Somewhere around four in the morning, our power went out. My first thought when I woke up freezing was, "Oh, man, I didn't draw water." We were in a winter wonderland that was indeed beautiful, but Doug, my musician husband, had to play that night, and I had an empty bathtub.

Country girls can survive, though. As I was scraping icy snow off the deck to heat on the wood insert for washing, I heard a generator start up next door. I remembered, with regret, Doug's son had never returned the one we loaned him for his haunted trail at Halloween.

I heated two pots for washing - one for each of us. The water was only lukewarm, but bearable. For an old hippie who had lived in his '69 Econoline Van when he was on the road with a band, Doug sure had a problem with washing out of a pot. I guess hippies weren't necessarily country boys.

I held him by both shoulders and gave him the instructions passed from mother to daughter for several generations in my family - Wash as far down as possible. Wash as far up as possible. Then wash possible. He told me he had only planned to wash possible. I left him to it and went to dry my hair.

He finished suspiciously fast and came into the living room. I was putting a chair in front of the wood insert. "What are you doing?" he asked me.

"I'm going to put the fan in front of the heater and dry my hair like I did before we had those little hair dryers."

"We don't have a fan," he informed me.

"We have two in the basement," I scoffed.

"They run on electricity," he said, completely deflating my cowgirl up attitude.

Reasonably clean...well one of us was more reasonably clean than the other - we headed out. The town the dance was in only had rain, so there was no question of canceling. Getting out of Guilford County was the problem. We had to run an obstacle course.

To get to the interstate, Doug maneuvered around fallen trees, going off the road completely at times. After dodging falling ice and limbs for about a mile and a half, he came to a complete stop.

In front of us was a large tree, lying completely across the road. Other trees had broken its fall, so there was a space underneath. After a moment's contemplation, Doug went for it. Surprisingly, we made it to the dance before the rest of the band who lived in the town.

With one gig under our belt, we were waiting for word on the Saturday night one which was only one county over. With 175,000 people out of power, that one was certainly iffy. Getting information was difficult, though, because during the night our phone line went down.

I walked all around the Palmer estate with my cell phone. There must have been ice on some of the towers it bounced off because it flashed the no service icon. Finally, I found one small spot at the end of the driveway where I could get through.

The phone was ringing when Landon, Doug's seven-year-old grandson came from around the fence, shouting like a kamikaze pilot. I hurried back up the hill to see what was wrong. Landon was just letting off pent-up energy.

He and his dad had come to grandma's house next door when their power went out, and he had been cooped up far too long. Yes, we live next door to my husband's ex-wife. It has already been determined that I am eligible for sainthood. Grandma's power was out, too, but she had a generator.

I looked reluctantly back at the spot it had taken me so long to find, sighed and walked inside with him. Disappointed when we told him he couldn't play the Wii or watch Netflix, he then asked for food.

We didn't have much, but chocolate chip cookies are always welcome to a seven-year- old. Sitting at the table dipping them in milk, he said, "Man, you people should have a generator like Grandma? We're watching movies over there."

"When did grandma get a generator," Doug said, more to make

conversation than a need to know.

"She didn't," Landon responded, mouth full of cookie. "Dad loaned her his."

Living with Germophobics

My sister, Jennie, my husband, Doug, and my best friend, Barbara, suffer from the same problem. They're borderline germophobics. I say borderline because they don't wash their hands five times before sitting down to eat or open doors with a handkerchief. Even though Doug has been known to flush a public toilet with his foot, they aren't afraid of germs. They just don't like them.

I, on the other hand, am not in the least worried about germs. Doug has watched in horror as I cleaned a CD that's skipping by licking it. I thought I was being good by honoring the seven second rule when I drop food on the floor. Still they yell, "You're not going to eat that, are you?"

Odd as it may seem, given his attitude toward germs, I caught Doug washing the dog's bowls in the sink with my dish cloth. When I protested…. loudly… he gave me that ages old myth that dog's mouths are cleaner than human's.

I asked him how could that possibly be true. Dogs use their tongues as wash cloths as well as toilet paper, and they have a propensity for eating rotting animal flesh. He went to Snopes it while I bleached the sink and threw the dishcloth in the trash. He was disappointed to find I was right.

None of these three people I love have any faith in the cleanliness of restaurants. Closely examining dishes and silverware brings a frown to their brows. Their germaphobia runs rampant when eating out.

Doug and I were sharing a soda at Subway. We put two straws in the middle hole. When Doug took a sip, his nose touched the top of my straw. It's a big nose and does get in the way sometimes.

He apologized profusely and offered to get me another straw. I just laughed and reached for the cup. He stopped me, "I just can't let you use that straw after it's touched my nose."

"Does it bother you that much?" I asked.

"Yes, " he said solemnly, "It bothers me that much."

I smiled, pulled my straw out of the cup, turned it upside down and stuck it back in the cup. "There now," I told him, "Problem solved."

It's not just the dishes and silverware, though. Doug also hates for servers to sweep near him in restaurants. He covers his plate and glass with napkins until they finish. For some reason I can only blame on bad karma, this happens to him a lot.

When it happened for the umpteenth time last week I looked at him and said, "You need to give up. This is life, and you're going to have to eat some dirt."

The musician in him overcame the germophobic for a moment. He took his napkin off his glass, and said, "You know that would make a great country song."

Jennie and Barbara keep hand sanitizer companies in business. I have watched many times in amusement as Jennie wipes our entire table with sanitizer before allowing us to sit down. When her grandbabies were barely old enough to talk, they knew to reach in Nanny's purse and pull out the sanitizer to wipe their hands.

Barbara doesn't bother with the purse sized sanitizer. She keeps a quart jug of it on our table at one of the venues the band plays. After a rousing two-step where she changes partners several times, she not only wipes her arms and hands with it, she passes it to everyone else at the table and expects them to do the same. Because she's a nurse, they usually humor her.

Although restaurants are a big problem, my little germophobics have problems at home, too. Jennie was upset when asthma forced her to quit wiping everything down with bleach. Doug has such a problem with silverware being turned eating side up in the dish rack, he had it put in our wedding vows.

Doug always checks his dishes before using them and has accused me of washing them too fast. He may be right. He came back from his daily walk to find me zoned out. I had been sick, and the combination of not eating properly, plus medication, had affected my blood sugar.

He sat me up and fed me orange juice from a wide, heavy bourbon glass. When I came to my senses he was holding the glass to my mouth, urging me to finish the juice. My eyes focused on the thin circle of dried milk around the bottom of the almost empty glass.

My first clear thought was, "I hope he doesn't see that." My second clear thought was, "If he does, I hope he doesn't tell Barbara."

Because of our geographical locations, I never have to deal with Jennie, Doug, and Barbara at the same time. But I did have dinner with Barbara and Doug a few weeks ago. It made me smile to see both of them reach for plastic cutlery instead of the real silverware wrapped in a napkin.

I waited until they had started eating with their plastic utensils before saying, "I wonder if the people in the factories where they make those things wash their hands after going to the bathroom."

Cost of three people to eat at K&W - $17.83. Simultaneous look of horror on Barbara and Doug's face - Priceless!

Bra Burning

Choosing fashion over comfort should never be an option. Women are the most susceptible to this oddity. And, sadly, I think sex plays a large part in women's clothing designs. The underlying sex theme, of course, is most obvious when it comes to women's underwear. Thongs were invented by a FrenchMAN, and the founder of FREDERICKS of Hollywood invented the push-up bras.

Last month I rebelled.

It was bound to happen at some point. I am after all a child of the '60's. Rebellion was not encouraged in my home back then, but last week, a few decades late, I gathered up all my bras and headed for the outside trash can with them.

When I went by Doug, who was sitting on the deck reading, with my arms full of bras, he asked what I was doing. I told him not only were bras uncomfortable in general, the underwire variety was dangerous to boot. And I was fed up.

Doug didn't say anything until the end of the week. After all, he lived during the bra burning era, too. But when Friday was on the horizon he pointed out we had a gig, and being a woman of mature years, I probably needed to wear underclothes.

So, I ventured into the ridiculous world of fashion bras, brought home half a dozen and went to work with scissors, a serrated knife and pliers. I cut the more elaborate decorations off, then used the knife to saw through the sides and bottoms of the underwire ones to extract the wide piece of metal, not wire as we've been told.

When Doug walked in I was pulling one of the c-shaped pieces of metal out with the pliers. It came loose with a snap and almost hit me in the eye. Do you see what I'm talking about?" I told him using the pliers to shake the wire furiously in his direction. "Men did this to us!" "I get your point," he told me placatingly. "Now put the pliers down before you hurt one of us."

I finally conceded that, for propriety's sake, I need to wear bras, but at least I made a statement. If only in my own home. At this point I must add a disclaimer: This reflects only the attitude of me, the writer. My husband loves push-up bras. I think that alone proves my point.

Alcohol

There were people gathering below my house, an older couple, teenagers, a toddler holding her young mother's hand. Some came in cars, some on foot. I watched them from the picture window in my music room. For a moment, I was tempted to join them, but only for a moment. I didn't know these people. They were strangers.

"William, wake up. William, talk to me. William, why did you do that?"

That was what Doug and I heard, what made us hurry down our driveway the Sunday night before. There was a young man lying on the pavement. His girlfriend was holding his head, yelling at him. He was unresponsive. They had been drinking, she said. They had been fighting, she said. The two go together, don't they?

I looked at her boyfriend. I didn't see the blood on his forehead or the scrape on his side. Doug would tell me about them later. My eyes were focused on his stomach. It had started rising up and down in an exaggeration, almost a pantomime, of normal breathing.

My older brother used to do that with his stomach when we were kids. I never could. I knew this wasn't normal. I looked around, trying to conjure up someone to tell, but there was no one. Doug had gone back to the house to phone 911.

A passerby stopped. He pulled the girlfriend off the young man, told her she shouldn't be shaking him like that. Standing beside the unconscious young man, I looked at his face.

He was so young, probably not even old enough to drink.

"We had a ####ing fight," the girlfriend screamed to neither of us in particular. "He jumped out of the car. I hit him. Oh my God, I hit him."

I looked at the screaming, sobbing girl with smeared makeup, nose running. I looked at the man trying to calm her. My gaze returned to the boy's stomach rising and falling, run over by his own girlfriend, and I felt the futility of it all burning my throat and eyelids.

The first responder arrived. He knelt beside the boy. The stomach rose, went back down and was still. The first responder started chest compressions. The girl screamed louder. The passerby held her, tried to calm her.

I walked over to the stop sign, skirting a tall can of something alcoholic and one of the boy's shoes.

I wanted to grab the screaming girl, pick up the poor lifeless child on the pavement, take them back in time, pull the alcohol out of their hands, and pour it down a drain.

Instead, I leaned against the stop sign and wrapped my arms around it, felt the roughness of the wood against my face, watched what was left in the can he had been drinking from run down the pavement and into the culvert.

Three days later people I didn't know gathered below my house, mourning the young man I had watched die. And though a glass separated me from them, I cried with them.

Their tears were for a friend, a son, a brother. Mine were because I knew... Without a doubt I knew... With every ounce of my being I knew... We will never learn... We will never, ever learn.

Good Music Will do That to You

I was listening to Conway Twitty while I cleaned house one morning. Doug was in his workshop in the basement rebuilding a steel guitar for a customer. He came up for lunch, listened to Conway with me while he ate, then went back to the basement.

I was busy with a cleaning project, so didn't join him for lunch. I had also skipped breakfast. Not a good thing to do since I have diabetes. After he went back to the basement I started getting that low blood sugar feeling and ate a small candy bar.

The candy didn't do the trick, so I drank a glass of orange juice. Doug came back up from the basement while I was drinking the orange juice. I was almost back to normal, but still a bit dazed, and didn't answer him when he spoke to me.

He took one look at me, walked me to the couch, got a blanket to cover me with and turned the TV to my favorite Netflix program. After he had me settled, he kissed the top of my head and said, "That's it. No more Conway for you, young lady."

I Fell in Love Again Last Night

Someone asked me recently at what point I fell in love with Doug. I hadn't planned to, just wanted to have fun. But on our first date, I noticed a thick book about Van Gogh in his back seat. I found out he not only loved to read, he painted too. That was my first hint there was more to this tall, long-legged musician than just his music.

I guess I knew instinctively there was a chance he might upset my comfortable, happy life down there in Cheraw, South Carolina. So, after a couple of dates I told this funny, talented, good-looking, extremely intelligent man (who was willing to drive two hours just to see me) that I didn't want to see him anymore.

He was sitting on my front porch steps at the time. He patted the step beside him and said, "Can we talk about it?"

No man had ever said that to me. I was intrigued. I sat down. We talked. I kept seeing him.

But the defining moment for me was in his car on the way to a gig. We were having one of our animated conversations when he used a four-syllable word. AND he used it in the proper context. I'm a writer. That made my heart go ahhhh.

A couple of months ago we were on our way to the Monroe Shrine Club, a long drive for us. Doug was trying a different way. Halfway down, he turned left at a stop light and said, "We've been this way before. I remember this plethora of eating places."

Yep. Plethora.......used correctly.

Every time he does that I fall in love with him all over again.

Open to Interpretation

Doug and I have a bi-denominational marriage. He's a Methodist. I'm a Baptist. The differences in our religious upbringing are subtle and seldom show. Though, he was pleasantly surprised when he played in a Baptist Church with his gospel band, and they received a love offering, a common thing in Baptist Churches. He said, "That's a mighty big tip."

However, our denominational difference was really telling when a song called *The Baptism of Jesse Taylor* came on the radio. For those of you who aren't fans of older country music, it's a song about the meanest man in town who got right with the Lord, joined the church and was baptized. Easy interpretation, right?

When it finished playing, Doug said, "That's a good song. You know they drowned that son of a gun."

After I stopped laughing, I corrected him, "Jesse Taylor got saved, Doug."

He shook his head and said, "Weren't you listening? They held him under the water until he drowned, and everyone cried hallelujah when Satan lost a good right arm."

In Doug's defense I think his interpretation was based on his head-sprinkling Methodist experience. We Baptists know what that head under the water means.

Ghosts

Thanksgiving has always been my favorite holiday. Even more than Christmas. I've been celebrating it at my house since I was nineteen. But this year, at Aaron and Tina's request, I have passed the torch.

An old tradition comes to an end.

A new tradition begins.

So, today my house is quiet. But I feel the ghosts of Thanksgiving past – chief among them my kids - scampering around me. Stealing cherries off the banana split cake when they think I'm not looking, grabbing a boiled egg while I'm checking the turkey, lying around the living room watching the parades. They never sat on the couch - I always had to step over them.

Here in the quietness, their noisy, happy chatter resonates down the corridors of my mind, growing more and more distant as the hours pass. My little ghosts. On the perimeter of my vision, just out of sight, talking all at once, excited without knowing why they're excited.

This year I will miss hearing the same questions the four of them ask every Thanksgiving.

Aaron: "Did you put giblets in the giblet gravy?" I make him a special one without giblets. He calls it his non-giblet giblet gravy.

Kevin: "Does the banana split cake have pineapple in it?" He has asked this question for over thirty years.

DeAnne: "Are you going to make my vegetarian dressing?" I've been doing that since she was fourteen.

Tony: "Does the potato salad have onions in it?" I make two versions.

There are lots more ghosts with me today - not just my children. A lifetime of family and friends populate the Thanksgivings of my memory. They came and are still here or, for all kinds of reasons, stayed awhile and left.

To the ghosts of Thanksgiving past - living and dead - who on this day drift gently across my mind - I miss you all. I loved you all. Happy Thanksgiving.

Virtual Reality

We got our first computer about thirty years ago. It was an Apple. The internet had not yet been commercialized, so I am not sure why my husband bought the computer. Technologically speaking, he wasn't farsighted, and I never saw him use his purchase.

In the general confusion of our divorce, I ended up with the computer. I also ended up with our two sons and daughter, and since they were the only ones who used the computer, it was fitting that we retained custody of it.

I give that computer the credit for Aaron and Kevin's career choices. Aaron is a program developer, and Kevin's job has many titles, but they all mean he's responsible for the anything to do with computers in his company.

Other computers followed the apple, and we eventually got the early crude version of today's internet. I was not interested in computers, never touched any of them. However, the terminology the boys used stuck in my brain.

When I ambitiously applied for a computer job in a grocery store in the nineties, I got it. The interviewer told his superior I was computer literate. I was elated. The panic didn't set in until they left me alone with the computer and a thick instruction book.

The book didn't help. I had never turned a computer on, couldn't work a mouse, or a printer, and had no idea how to insert a floppy disc. These people expected me to control all the scanning and inventory in the store. Only one day in and I deleted the whole produce department.

I didn't think it was necessary to tell my manager what I had done - no need for two people in the office to be hyperventilating. I called Aaron in California. He talked me through it. It took me six hours to undelete the thousands of items I had trashed. I felt like Lucy in the chocolate factory without Ethel.

I have learned quite a bit more about computers since then, and almost a decade ago I discovered Facebook. I loved Facebook and amassed a multitude of friends. Then Doug and I became victims of internet stalking.

The three ladies doing it were older than us and not computer savvy, so it was more humorous than harmful. Their Facebooks were open, so we could see every move they made and counteract it.

The harassment became so bad, we had to ban them from the band's website and Facebook, block them from our personal Facebook pages as well as both our e-mails. Still they persisted, tricking people who were our Facebook friends into giving them our personal information, pictures and videos.

Because of this, I decided to decrease the number of friends I had on Facebook to a more manageable amount. I started with people who had a blank profile picture. Most of these were deactivated accounts anyway. I then got rid of those who had thousands of friends. They wouldn't notice my absence.

Next, I unfriended people whose names I didn't recognize. Several delete buttons too late, I discovered I had unfriended cousins, nieces and nephews because I didn't recognize their names. I even unfriended my son. I recognized his name, but he had deactivated his account and didn't have a photo. Fair is fair.

I unfriended my children's friends from high school and work and people with whom I never interacted. I deleted those who hadn't posted on their page in months. I unfriended people who posted nothing but recipes, because I was on a diet. Those recipes undermined my will power.

After almost a month, losing a lot of friends and quite a few relatives in the process, I completed my mission. I had unfriended over a thousand people.

Still I spend too much time on the internet. In fact, just this week my husband Doug told me he has decided to let my funeral plans reflect my love of technology. He said he's giving me an e-funeral.

I thought of all those people who are no longer my friends. I'm going to be sending out friend requests again. I have to build my friend list back up. Otherwise, I won't have any virtual mourners at my virtual funeral.

Fifty Different Shades of Gray

I told my son, Aaron, I was going to write a column about fifty shades of gray. He said, "Mom, you know that's porn, don't you?" I told him I was using the American spelling of gray, and my column was about growing older, not sex.

The earliest and most prominent sign of growing older is the changing color of our hair. Even though I dye mine, underneath I am still gray. Gray haired people used to be revered for their wisdom, but the young aren't interested in wisdom anymore.

Unlike Solomon, it is down low on their hierarchy of needs. As soon as the gray hits, we are moved to their uninteresting list. I understand this attitude because my own dad's hair had turned white before I was born. I didn't realize how interesting he was until years after he died.

Just as there are fifty shades of gray to our hair, there are even more shades to the lives we lived in mainstream society. We were business owners, nurses, doctors, lawyers, musicians, writers, highway patrolmen, cops, teachers, military personnel, parents, and children.

In a lifetime of living we have survived the loss of jobs, homes, money, love, friends, and family. We have been on top of the world and on the bottom of the stack. What experience we would bring to problem solving. But no one cares. Any shade of gray makes us generic and cloaks us in anonymity.

My kids and I received a valuable lesson in profiling the elderly a few years ago. We were visiting with my mom in the dining room of her nursing home when a nondescript resident wheeled slowly by us. There was no way to tell what sort of man he had been physically.

Age and illness had taken their toll, and he was a shrunken version of whatever he had once been. No one paid him any attention. The home was populated with wheelchairs, and his was just one more.

A church group was setting up for service and a little bit of chaos surrounded them. He wheeled around the chaos and headed for the piano in the back of the room.

While my children's happy chatter floated in the air around me, I watched him with a feeling of sadness. Sadness for him, my mom, and all the people who inhabited those halls.

The pastor/singer followed my gaze, then looked back at me. Wordlessly, we communicated our pity for this tiny man as he wended his way toward the goal. He finally reached it, and one of my kids ran to move the piano bench out of his way.

He touched the keys tentatively with a thin hand. Making contact with the keys transformed him. He sat straighter, grew taller and more confident. Those thin hands, graceful now, played the most beautiful rendition of "How Great Thou Art" I have ever heard.

He played a few more songs, gaining the attention of and holding in his thrall everyone in the room. When his impromptu performance was over, I invited him to our table. My kids plied him with questions.

We learned he had played with musical greats back in the day before returning home to teach music. Such an amazing man wheeling himself through the halls of the local nursing home. I have never forgotten the beautiful music he shared with us that day. I was honored to be in his audience.

Even though I've managed to stave it off for years, I am the one growing older now, and I feel the anonymity seeping in. Fortunately, I like it. As does my musician husband who once toured and recorded with the country music stars.

Doug was on more TV shows than he can remember and played to crowds whose numbers ranged from fifteen thousand to two-hundred thousand before leaving life on the road to settle down in Greensboro. What people see now is a white-haired man in Converse shoes and faded jeans shopping in Food Lion.

I'm not complaining, though. Like an irresponsible babysitter, I have left the youngsters home and am enjoying the heck out of my life. Fridays and Saturdays find me dancing...always dancing.

Doug, of course, is on stage playing while I dance. He's not as retired as I am, but he's doing what he loves. My friends don't care what I did in another lifetime. I am no longer identified by my occupation. I am liked or not liked based on my personality and character alone. Retirement is a great leveler.

The next time you see a gray-haired woman or man sitting alone, say hello. Sit down and talk to them for awhile. You will probably be amazed at what they've done. Remember the color gray does have many shades, and they're all interesting.